HOMER

THE SMALL-TOWN BASEBALL ODYSSEY

Jeff Karzen

 **August Publications**

Minneapolis, Minnesota

Homer: The Small-Town Baseball Odyssey

August Publications
527 Marquette Av., Suite 800
Minneapolis, MN 55402
612.343.5207
augustpublications.com

ISBN 978-0-9752706-5-3

9 8 7 6 5 4 3 2 1

Editor: Jim Robins
Designer (cover and interior): Natalie Nowytski

TABLE OF CONTENTS

This book is for my parents, Ron and Marilyn Karzen, who instilled in me the love of sports (dad) and books (mom). It's also for all the people in small towns all over this country just like Homer, who dream of one day having the spotlight on them — just for a moment. Hang in there. You never know when your time will come.

And lastly, for everyone who still believes that the great game of baseball remains America's Pastime.

Acknowledgements

This book simply would not have been written without the cooperation from many different people. There's no way to thank everyone here, but I'll do my best to dole out appropriate credit.

First, a big thank you to the good people of Homer. Growing up in Chicago, we'd always hear people say that small-town folks are nicer than their big-city counterparts. Without alienating my fellow Chicagoans, let's just say people in Homer are darn nice. From village manager Jerry Stonebreaker inviting me to chat in his backyard garden to Gale Smith allowing me to pepper him with questions in the barbershop, everyone was more than accommodating to this unfamiliar journalist invading their tidy village.

Thanks to Mike Warner for letting me run amok in his *Homer Index* archive books. Thanks to my friend and awesome photographer Doug Allen for all your great action shots and scene-setting looks of Homer's downtown. Thanks to all the former players I interviewed for talking openly and honestly. Thanks to Chuck Finch for telling his side of the story and doing it passionately.

Thanks to John Johnson at the Michigan High School Athletic Association for making time in your ridiculously busy schedule and granting us use of some of the MHSAA's great photos. Thanks also to the *Battle Creek Enquirer, Detroit News,* and Spring Arbor University for allowing your photos to be used.

Enormous thanks to Scott Salow. You'll be glad to know that I won't be calling or emailing at strange hours anymore with random questions about a minute detail from a game four years ago. I greatly appreciate your patience and diligence in answering all of my questions. When this book was still in the infant stages, before there was a publisher on board, Salow would take time from his busy schedule to meet me halfway at the Stagecoach Inn in Marshall where I'd run my tape recorder for up to an hour, just getting a rough sketch of information down.

Last, but certainly not least, I need to thank my personal (and unpaid) editors. Lots of you took the time to scan some pages, but nobody took as much of it as Jenny, Ryan, and Mom. Jenny, thank you so much for allowing me to vent and think out loud about this project over the last year. It was overwhelming at times, but having you by my side was a calming influence that I couldn't have survived without. The fact that you've been a copy editor for the last five years didn't hurt either! You're the best.

Ryan, you should be doing this for a living, man. You're a great editor and sounding board. Thanks a ton for your suggestions and attention to detail.

Mom, this book had better get a prominent spot in your expansive library (I mean house). Hopefully, editing it didn't keep you off your 150-book-per-year pace. Along with being a voracious reader, you're a super editor too. Thanks a million.

Foreword

It was less than 48 hours after Homer had won the Division 3 baseball state championship, and I found myself sitting in the junior-high principal's office.

I had spent much of my time in school sitting in the principal's office, but there was always a nun or two involved, a paddle, and a lecture about how I was going to grow up and amount to nothing. They weren't too far off, but that's another story. This time I was in the principal's office to visit with Scott Salow, Homer's baseball coach and junior-high principal, not necessarily in that order.

Two days before that, I had asked Salow where he would be Monday morning, and he told me he would be in his office at school. I found that funny because his team had just won a second state title in three years, and most coaches I know who might accomplish something like that would take a week or two off, or at least call in sick for a few days.

But no, Salow insisted, he would be at work and therefore I was, too. I was there to write a story on Salow because we were honoring him as the *Detroit Free Press*'s 2006 Prep Person of the Year.

The Prep Person of the Year idea came several years earlier from a former fellow prep writer. He handled the assignment for the first few years and then decided he was too big in the business and went on scholarship. That left it up to me if we were going to continue the feature. To be honest, it would have been fine with me to just dump the idea and head for vacation once the baseball and softball tournaments were over.

But this was an excellent way for us to honor someone who has done something extraordinary in the world of high-school athletics. All of the winners have been coaches, with one exception. Dathan Riztenhein, who was Michigan's greatest distance runner of all time and has gone on to become an Olympic athlete, received the award after his senior year at Rockford.

This is an award I take incredibly seriously. The recipient has to have accomplished something remarkable, but he or she must be a person of tremendous character. Sorry, but if you're someone I wouldn't want one of my kids to play for or associate with, you've got no chance at this award.

To be honest, I didn't know Scott that well before deciding on him for the award. I had only met him a few times, but there was something about him I immediately liked. I was impressed by him and by many of his players. They were a bunch of class kids from this small town, and I believed that to be a reflection on Salow. He certainly had the credentials — helping Homer to two state titles, a national record 75-game winning streak and 113 victories in 115 games — is one of the great achievements in the history of Michigan high-school athletics. To me, it ranks right up there with Saginaw Arthur Hill's amazing 1973 football team that outscored its nine opponents 443-0, which came two years before the state playoffs began.

And he did it at this small town that could be anywhere in America, but is right here in Michigan.

The day after Homer won the 2006 title, I was speaking with a friend, Mike Dempsey, and I told him Salow was going to be our Prep Person of the Year. Mike had been in Battle Creek to see Grosse Pointe North play. The North game was just after the Homer game, and as he waited, he heard a small group of men complaining about Salow. "They were killing your boy," Dempsey said, referring to Salow, which made me worry about my selection.

And then I sat there that morning and listened to Scott talk about his days as a college baseball player and benchwarmer and how he became a coach, just like his college coach, Hank Burbridge. He spoke about how he nearly lost the baseball coaching job when he became middle-school principal and a small faction of people wanted him gone. But the vast majority of people in town, as well as his players, rallied around him at a school-board meeting. He talked about losing the state championship game in 2005 and how much time he spent in the offseason with the losing pitcher from that game.

That's when I knew I had the right guy for our Prep Person of the Year. When we finished some two hours later, I told Scott what a fascinating story it was. "It would make a good book, wouldn't it?" he asked.

Yes, it would. Yes, it did.

That brings us to this book, written by Jeff Karzen. Jeff has never been convicted of anything, but I think we can convict him of writing a pretty darn good book. He does an excellent job of describing this amazing three-year run for these amazing players and their amazing coach. But he goes far beyond writing about just a high-school baseball team. He transports you into the middle of this quaint little town where everyone knows your name — and everything else you ever did in your life.

When you read the part about the school board meeting where the people stand up for Scott, you can almost imagine Gene Hackman playing the role of Scott in baseball's version of "Hoosiers."

Reading about the 2006 quarterfinal victory over Beal City was kind of like watching the movie "Apollo 13." You know it's going to end well, but you have to keep reading just to make sure.

For years I've hoped someone would ask me to give them a quote about their book to put on the cover. One of those quotes like: "If you read only one book this year, make it this one!" The quote I've always wanted to give is: "I haven't read this book, but if I did I would probably like it." Well, I will have to wait to give that quote to someone else. I have read this book and I like it — very much.

Mick McCabe
Detroit Free Press

Photo by Doug Allen.

Talent and Tension

For five innings of baseball, the outcome seemed obvious. With rain one minute, bright sunshine the next, the streak appeared destined to fall on this late afternoon in June of 2005. Homer High School's baseball team finally met its match when a gritty group of Blissfield Royals took the field in a lose-and-you're-out quarterfinal playoff game.

Yet a couple of classic Homer breaks quickly changed the momentum faster than gusts of wind on a goofy-weathered summer Michigan day. When a Homer batter's strikeout miraculously turned into the game's tying run, everyone in the 1,000-plus crowd knew who was going to win. After all, this was Trojans baseball. The victory over tradition-rich Blissfield added to Homer's mystique and earned it a precious national record of 74 straight triumphs. Two games remained for back-to-back state championships, but the conclusion would be as unpredictable as ever. And the entire village of 1,800 in Homer, Michigan, came along for the adventure. Crazy thing is, the coach in charge of it all almost was not there.

From the beginning, there was something different about Homer baseball. So many great players all in the same age group, all playing their natural positions. How unusual a situation to never wonder from game to game who would play catcher, who would be at second base, etc. For almost four straight years, coach Scott Salow penciled in nearly the same lineup every game. While the faltering car industry had put Michigan's economy in a freefall, Homer baseball gave their tidy village something to smile about. Elsewhere, basketball and football had won over the hearts of America's youth, but in this small town nestled in southern Michigan, baseball remained America's Pastime.

Homer won big and did it with flair. But to the coaches, respecting the game was just as important as winning. Scott and Tom Salow, Homer's coaches past and present, learned the game from Michigan small-college legend Hank Burbridge. Under Burbridge, the Salow brothers were taught the merits of hustling and hard work and how it translated to victories. Homer's players were expected to hustle and then hustle some more. This wasn't just running hard for the sake of running. The Salows reasoned that they were in the business of character building, not just winning baseball games. Judging by Homer's success on and off the field, they were doing quite well on both accounts.

For all of the players' considerable talents, they developed a work ethic to match. Perhaps it was because they were from a one-stoplight town or maybe it was just a product of Homer's individual personalities. But whatever the reasons, Homer boys had a hard-working ethos befitting their blue-collar town. Naturally, it was well received in the community. In this everybody-knows-everybody town, Homer baseball developed a cult following. Players

COACH AND MENTOR HANK BURBRIDGE AT SPRING ARBOR, FLANKED BY SCOTT AND TOM SALOW (RIGHT). PHOTO COURTESY OF THE SALOW FAMILY.

couldn't go anywhere without being asked questions about the most recent games — not that they minded. Individual accolades, record-shattering performances, and an unbelievable winning streak were just some of the moments that would define this amazing era of Homer baseball.

The small town wasn't immune to controversy, though. At the center of the debate was Scott Salow, the coach who loved his players and was winning at an impressive clip. In the middle of the records and playoff runs, though, Salow's job was in jeopardy. When Salow became a school administrator, the question arose over whether he could continue his duties as the varsity baseball coach. Would he stay or would he go? Who would coach the talented players? The case came to a head at a charged board meeting, where emotions ran high and the fate of Homer's highly successful coach hung in the balance.

>>><<<

The phone call came around 9 p.m. Scott Salow picked it up and immediately knew something was wrong. The school's superintendent was on the other end, and this wasn't a "Hi, how're ya doing?" call. Instead, it would shape the next 14 months of Salow's life in a way he never could have imagined. All Salow ever wanted to do was coach baseball. Teaching at Homer Middle School proved rewarding too, but Salow was, and is, a baseball coach. Judging by Homer's record, he was a darn good coach, too. But when Salow tried to make the move to administrator, everything changed. When Brent Holcomb, Homer's superintendent, called the Salow home that September night in 2003, he had a biting quandary for Salow to think about.

"He said there was good news and bad news," Salow said. "And when he said they were offering me the principal job but … my jaw just hit the floor."

Superintendent Holcomb did indeed offer Salow the middle-school principal job. But it was much more complicated than that. Because of a controversial decision by Homer's hiring committee that was backed by the superintendent, Holcomb delivered the excruciatingly difficult news to Salow. He could be the principal. But, he'd have to give up the baseball job. Salow was shocked. Stunned. His mind raced to his baseball kids who were like family. He thought of all the hours spent together during the traditional spring-break bonding week when Homer baseball players aren't allowed to leave town; no Cancun or Jamaica for them. Instead, there was baseball practice with fun sprinkled in. Sometimes, Salow would take them to a Detroit Tigers game or invite them to his house to watch the NCAA men's basketball championship game, which always falls on the Monday of Homer's break. All these great times and experiences rushed through Salow's brain as a major decision hung in the balance.

Salow tossed and turned that night inside his farm-style house in Concord, a corn-stalked community about 10 miles east of Homer in southern Michigan. He didn't know what to do. At the age of 34, his life seemed to be in order. There was his wife, Cammy, the love of his life and his support system during all the inevitable hours that consumed him as a coach. The chance to earn a middle-school principal salary of $70,000 would allow Cammy to work fewer hours as a nurse at the hospital. That way, she could spend more time with the couple's two young daughters, ages 9 and 6. Still, Salow couldn't get baseball out of his mind. He had a short time to make a choice that would affect the next several years of his life.

"It's easy to say it was one of the hardest [phone calls] I've ever had to make," Holcomb later said. "There was disappointment on my part. I could tell there was disappointment on his part, and some reluctance. On my part, there were regrets all along, 'Are you doing the right thing?' And I think you always feel that as an administrator. I wasn't sure what decision he would make."

The next morning, Salow showered, put on his shirt, tie, and pants like he always did and arrived at work at his customary 6:30 a.m. But this was not every other day. Salow walked down the hallway before school started and told Holcomb he would accept the principal job. Baseball, the sport he cherished since growing up playing catch with his grandfather, would have to take a backseat to professional advancement. Shortly after accepting the middle-school principal job, Salow's life turned crazy. It was just the beginning of a surreal string of events.

>>><<<

Chuck Finch is an influential man in Homer. A longtime schoolteacher, Finch has been an assistant coach on the high school's baseball and football teams for more than 20 years. In addition, he is a former union president of 12 years and a longtime member of the Homer Education Association, the teachers' union. A small man with an intimidating demeanor and presence, Finch is a take-no-crap individual. Never a great athlete, Finch wasn't out of shape but his adult league fast-pitch baseball days had come to an end. While he has his core group of supporters in town, he's also been known to rub some others the wrong way. And don't expect him to apologize for it either. Finch's youngest child, C.J., was a top athlete at Homer and the starting second baseman and leadoff hitter on the baseball team. After serving as head coach on the junior-varsity team for a number of years, the elder Finch decided he wanted to coach C.J. for his last three years of high school.

When Salow accepted the principal job, Finch and other influential members of the Homer Educational Association were quick on the baseball coach's trail. Finch told Salow it would be best if he promptly submitted a formal written resignation. That way, the ball could get rolling for Homer to get a new baseball coach well before the talent-rich team began its season. Chuck Finch thought there was only one person best suited for this job. One person who could lead the Trojans to their first-ever Michigan state championship. One person who would get every last ounce of talent out of the great group of players that Homer was bringing back. Chuck Finch even boasted to people around school and at a board meeting, "This is my job."

Salow began his principal job in September '03. In turn, Finch got his wish — sort of. Salow formally resigned from the head baseball post. The conflicted coach didn't feel good about the developments, far from it. Before his life was turned upside down, Salow thought this was going to be a seminal year on the diamond. Entering his fourth season at the helm, a special group of seven returning starters would be on this year's team. Five players in that group started as freshmen on a 30-4 varsity team, including C.J. Finch.

Add to that two tremendous seniors, including record-setting pitcher Josh Collmenter, and Salow's team looked ready for major things. But it was hard to think about baseball now. Small-town politics were at work, and the dominos were just starting to fall. In November, a letter circulated around town that alleged Salow and his older brother, Tom (Homer's high school principal and the varsity baseball coach before Scott), were ruining Homer's reputation.

The following is a portion of an unsigned letter mailed to select Homer residents:

Attention Homer Community Tax Payers:

Who is leading our schools? As parents of children in the Homer community, we have recently begun to ask ourselves this question. Two years ago, we ignored the fact that a new high school principal was hired without conducting an interview, or without posting the position. We later came to find out that this administrator does not have the proper credentials to lead our high school. He does not have a Master's degree, a requirement in the majority of Michigan schools. A few weeks ago, a search for a middle school principal was conducted. Four internal candidates, who are teachers in the Homer school district, were interviewed. Three of these teachers held Master's degrees, one held only a Bachelor's degree. To our shock, the superintendent chose the least qualified candidate, a candidate with only a teaching certificate, to fill the middle school principal position. Additionally, the middle school principal is the brother of the high school principal. Obviously we are running our school on the "buddy system," by not choosing the most qualified and educated candidate.

The one-page letter went on to say the school board and superintendent were making a mockery of the educational system. It ended by stating, *"Why are we paying the unqualified to*

lead our schools? The next time a bond issue comes up for a vote, we will remember that our school district is mismanaging its funds."
— *Parents For Better Schools Committee*

The letter hit Scott and Tom Salow like a rack of aluminum baseball bats. The cowardly nature of its anonymity also was disconcerting. "Who did this? What do they have against us?" the Salows asked. "That hurt more than anything else," Scott Salow said. "Both of us felt that we contributed a lot to Homer. That really hurt. My first thought was that I don't belong in Homer. We both talked about resigning. But we said we couldn't quit because that's the easiest thing to do. Tom was devastated. I think it hurt him more than me."

Scott Salow has his theories on who authored the letter but didn't know for sure. He's not sure he ever wants to know. As time passed, Salow altered his view on the situation. For two-plus months, he watched as former and current players and their families attended board meetings on his behalf. Salow realized this was about more than just him. The more he thought about not coaching baseball, the more he wanted to coach baseball. He couldn't give it up. Not now. In December 2003, Homer High School officially posted the job of head varsity baseball coach. Just before the 3 p.m. deadline on the last day applications were being accepted, Chuck Finch submitted his resume to the athletic director. So did head football coach Rob Heeke, one of Finch's friends. But there was one more candidate that altered the whole hiring process.

Scott Salow wanted his job back.

Understanding that it was one job or the other, Salow chose baseball. He would go back to teaching fifth-grade reading. That wasn't so bad anyway. He liked the kids — hell, loved the kids — and baseball would be back in his life. Salow's fifth-graders cried when he left to take the principal job. Now, he could be back with them and all their wonderful youthfulness, organizing pen pal projects, and watching them act out silly plays. "One job I had known my whole life and one I had done for three months," he said. "Based on that, baseball was going to win."

Salow sent out an email to his middle-school staff, saying he was resigning from the principal post. He also sent Holcomb a copy, adding that he'd return to the classroom (if only it were that easy). In a small rural town like Homer, keeping secrets is slightly harder than trespassing on White House property. Rumblings had already begun about Salow and it got worse.

"I remember it just being awkward walking around school," Salow said. "It felt as if all eyes were on me. It had kind of an eerie feeling to it." Students made colorful posters and taped them to the hallway walls, backing Salow for both duties. Petitions were going around school with dozens of signatures to keep Salow. Feeling uncomfortable with all the attention, Salow tore the posters down and hid them in his office. A board meeting was scheduled where Salow would formally announce his resignation as principal. The night before the meeting, Salow wrote his resignation letter in his home office.

Everywhere around him in the second-floor carpeted office were baseball memories, either from Homer or his playing days at Monroe High School and Spring Arbor University. Salow wouldn't let his wife Cammy read the letter because he wanted it to be personal. When he left the room, she snuck upstairs and read it anyway just to see what her husband was prepared to say.

Around 8 p.m. the following night, Salow walked across the school parking lot and into the side door of the elementary-school gymnasium. Homer's board meetings are usually held in a smaller media center, but with a hot-button item on this night's agenda, the meeting was moved to a bigger venue. "When I got to the gym, I just saw a mass of people," Salow recalled. "The next things I remembered seeing were the signs. They disappeared from my office. Sometime that night they disappeared."

Salow sat in the first row next to his brother and stared straight ahead. After a few minutes, it was his turn to speak. Salow tried to keep his emotions in check, but he was a man speaking from the heart. Tears started to flow as he said his piece. "It was hard, and basically the gist of it was that regardless of what happens tonight I hope to leave here as a teacher and coach and I take great pride in that," Salow said. "I expected and was prepared to keep the baseball job and go back to teaching. That's what I thought would come out of that night."

"If you were to listen to his letter of resignation and the emotion that came out and the sincerity with which Scott expressed himself, that was really tough," Holcomb said. "The thing that I saw from Scott was when the situation developed where there was some adversity surrounding him coaching; I think he handled that as well as anybody. What I found out about Scott was that his values and principles didn't waver."

After the coach delivered his speech, the community spoke and spoke loudly. A packed gym had listened. Those who were there said about 30 people stood and talked that night. Only two were against Salow being both a principal and coach. Players past and present spoke. Parents spoke. Teachers spoke. Plain old townsfolk spoke. There was one common theme: Scott Salow is a great coach, a great leader of young people, and capable of doing whatever duties are put in front of him. "Usually you don't hear that stuff until you're dead," Salow said. "Now I was hearing it when I'm 34 years old. What a night."

"Any time you have a packed gymnasium and such emotion, you're never sure which way it's going to swing," Holcomb said. "That was probably one of the best board meetings I've ever attended. The community got up and spoke. That's what a board meeting is supposed to be."

Within minutes the board had a decision. The vote was 7-0 in favor of Salow being baseball coach. Minutes later, the board voted 7-0 to not accept Salow's resignation as principal. He would assume both jobs after all. None of this sat well with Chuck Finch and his contingent on the HEA. They vowed to make sure their voice was heard too.

Prior to the eventful board meeting, the union's hiring committee thought it had a deal with Holcomb that it was one job or the other for Salow. "That did not sit well with a lot of the teachers," said Art Welch, a member of Homer's teachers' union for more than 30 years. "Part of it was that promises were made and then reneged on. It was really a slap in the face of the teachers, and a lot of people were irritated by that."

As the calendar flipped to 2004, Salow began to settle into his role as middle-school principal. The long hours he anticipated were even longer. Performing this duty at a small school means being counselor, head of the free and reduced lunch program, and standardized-testing coordinator in addition to the standard principal functions. But he attacked the job as if it were a tough ballgame, never wavering on giving his due diligence. It was only a month or so later when a new issue arose. Chuck Finch wasn't done with this matter. He filed a grievance against Salow's title of principal and varsity coach.

Baseball was set to begin in just three months, and Salow couldn't help but think, "Here we go again."

Just before the season began, Chuck Finch and the HEA took their grievance to a special board meeting. Finch was incensed at the situation. "Homer has always had a policy of not hiring a coach if he is an administrator," Finch later said. While that's not exactly right, Finch was fighting the good fight. In the 1980s and early '90s, then-Superintendent Lee Robinson also coached boys' and girls' cross-country. But, Finch contended, that's because nobody else wanted to be the coach. Holcomb himself helped coach J.V. football in the past. Regardless, Finch was in this fight for the long haul, and if nothing else, it was going to be long.

Finally, Salow was back with his boys. For two hours of practice out on the field after school, the coach could finally be just that. A coach. He could do so without thinking about the ugly politics that had recently entered his world. The players acted like nothing had happened. Sure, they knew the whole story. You'd be hard-pressed to find someone in Homer's tidy village that didn't know every sliver of the town's gossip. Still, all the athletes wanted was to play baseball. And, boy, these kids could play.

Just a month into the '04 season, Homer took claim of the No. 1 ranking in Division 3, the state's second-smallest classification. The Trojans were rolling, and Salow had his safe place. On the baseball field, he was back in his element, coaching and instructing young men on baseball, the sport that was part of his character since adolescence.

A magical season lay ahead. By all accounts, Homer was expecting the ride of a lifetime. Unfortunately, ugly words like *grievance* and *arbitrator* would also be part of the equation. Salow coached every game like it was his last. Unlike most coaches who profess to do the same, Salow really didn't know how much longer he'd be coach.

To a novice, the game of baseball is a simple one. You hit, run, pitch, catch, and in between, spit and scratch. Of course, that's far from the true meaning of the game that dates back to the 1800s. For those who play or coach or simply love baseball, there is a moment in time when you realize your philosophy on the game. Like fashion, the styles of baseball have come full circle. In the old days when home runs were rare, small ball emphasized bunting, and execution reigned supreme. Swinging for the fences has become the recent trend, but there's always going to be lovers of the small-ball theory. Ask any coach and he'll tell you where he learned his preferred style of ball, how he came to love it, and why it's the best. Scott Salow is no different. Salow would never let you think he invented the style, but he loves it all the same.

It could be argued that the foundation for Homer baseball starts with the "seven-second rule" or "Seven Factor." The unusual tactic embodies the spirit of baseball both Salow brothers learned at Spring Arbor University in Spring Arbor, Michigan, about 20 miles east of Homer, where they played under legendary NAIA coach Hank Burbridge. The Salows talk with reverence about their days under Burbridge, Scott as a bit player and Tom as a starter. Burbridge, who won more than 1,000 games at Spring Arbor, instilled an always-hustling mentality into the Salows that persists to this day. The seven-second rule is a simple one: When Homer makes its third out at the plate, every fielder must reach his position in the field by sprinting to reach it within seven seconds. When the Trojans are in the field, every player must find the dugout in seven seconds after the third out is made — no easy task for the right fielder sprinting to the third-base dugout.

"Our goal is to have our pitcher throw his first warm-up pitch before the opposing team is off the field," Scott said. "And it isn't unusual to see our opponents getting in the dugout, taking their time, and not have a batter ready when our pitcher has finished his warm-ups. If the umpire has to go into their dugout and ask for a batter, that's a win for Homer High School. When we come off the field, it is the goal of our leadoff hitter that inning to get his bat and helmet and be in the on-deck circle before the opposing pitcher throws his first warm-up pitch."

Homer's players bought into the crazy-hustle motives right from the beginning — perhaps because they didn't have a choice. Tom Salow took over the head-coaching duties at Homer in 1992 and established the ground rules. Scott says he had it easy: by the time he took over for his older brother in 2001 players knew what was expected of them. The days of bitching and moaning because of some perceived goofy policies were over. This is how it was done. Don't like it? Fine, you won't play. The philosophy that became the backbone of unprecedented success didn't end with the seven-second rule. When a pitch was fouled off during a game — either toward the backstop or down one of the foul lines — several Homer bench players immediately sprung from the dugout and darted after the ball. This became especially noticeable when the ball was fouled in front of an opponent's dugout. The opposing players would casually meander toward the foul ball, only to be passed by a rush of screaming Homer players. Some opposing coaches privately grumbled that this was going too far. They said this was showing up an opponent. But Homer didn't look at it that way. Too bad if you didn't like it. You probably didn't like losing 14-0 in five innings either.

"All the enthusiasm we brought to the table was unlike any other baseball team we ever played," said catcher Dale Cornstubble. "Nobody else hustles like us so we'd jump on them the very first inning. A kid from Reading [a conference rival] said it felt like we were up 2-0 before the game even started. It made you more pumped and made you excited to play if you hustled. It wasn't foolish at all."

These kids were just different than most high-school athletes. It's not that Salow was a baseball revolutionary who invented and concocted a new principle called "hustle." He had the players who were willing to do anything to win and better themselves and the team. The talented group of players all grew up in Homer, all playing baseball together on dusty fields in the hot summers. They liked each other almost as much as they liked winning. And by the time they reached high school, a little coaching and polishing turned very good individuals into a powerful, cohesive team.

"We tried to make it an exciting game because baseball can get long and boring, so we just tried to force the issue," pitcher Josh Collmenter said. "We liked to play with that enthusiastic mentality. So when you jump on teams like that and then get the momentum going before we throw the first pitch out, a lot of teams just folded. It kept everybody loose, kept everyone on their toes and didn't let us get stagnant."

Sure, the group had a few rebels, a few guys who wondered what all this extracurricular running had to do with baseball. But those heretics were drowned out by the larger group of players who loved everything Salow fed the boys. Dan Holcomb, the superintendent's son and one of five varsity four-year starters, was the brains of the operation. If high-school teams had a players' union representative, Homer's would've been the tall, athletic Holcomb. Holcomb thought the all-out hustle rules molded just fine into these one-stoplight country-town boys.

"[Salow] let us know right away that is the way it's going to be. If you don't like it, you can go down to J.V.," Holcomb said. "We bought into it real quick. As a freshman, you may have thought he just wanted you to hustle. But when you got older and were a junior or senior and younger guys were coming up behind you, you understood what he wanted from that. He wanted guys to fly around and have a good time and carry yourself, not necessarily with cockiness, but with a swagger and to be confident in yourselves. Once you got older you understood what Homer baseball was and why you have to buy into that and how it helps you." When the players' rep spoke, the teammates listened. So long as they weren't busy chasing down a foul ball.

Perhaps Homer's boys were built to be team-oriented players. Of course, they all had their individual talents and personalities, but the boys thrived on being a team. It's all they knew. It's how they were raised. It's not that cable television and indoor plumbing hadn't made its way to Homer, but the town breathes a sense of old-time, hard-working, no-nonsense living. Terrell Owens might be plastered all over ESPN, but that type of 21st century credo didn't jibe with Homer. The townsfolk hope it never does.

Take a drive down M-60 into the quaint little town of Homer and you might think somebody just plopped you into the middle of a Norman Rockwell painting. Turn off M-60 and onto Main Street (of course) and the two-block downtown looks like any stereotypical Small Town, USA. There's Gale's Barber Shop, Shrontz's Laundry Mat, Bernie's Bar, a post office, and the most distinguished building outside of the village, Cascarelli's Pizza, founded in 1935. "That's kind of the anchor of town," village manager Jerry Stonebreaker said. "Instead of Macy's, we have Cascarelli's."

PHOTO BY DOUG ALLEN

Located in the south-central portion of the state, Homer sits about 30 miles equidistant from Battle Creek and Jackson — the closest towns with a mall and any semblance of life past 9 p.m. Most people in Homer were born and raised there and have seen their children pass through the same Homer Middle and High School hallways that they did. People are friendly, traffic is non-existent, and it's the kind of town where you don't just know everybody, you know who they've dated, what block they live on, which sports they play, and what their parents and siblings do for a living. While the farming industry is dying off rapidly elsewhere this century, it remains the economic cornerstone in Homer. Corn and soybeans are the most common crops, and some dairy and cattle farms are also on the outskirts of town.

Jerry Stonebraker was a police officer in Southfield for 25 years when he retired from the force and decided, with his wife, to make a life change. Stonebraker wanted to move away from city life and find a place where he could relax after a lifetime of stressful work. Southfield isn't Los Angeles, but it is a Detroit suburb with a decent amount of frustrating highway traffic. The Stonebrakers settled on Homer, where Jerry would work as a broker at Citizens Bank while his wife, Daphne, opened a custom framing and gift gallery out of the house. In 2005, Stonebraker ran for village president (i.e. mayor) and won. By that time, he'd moved from Citizens Bank to become the human-resources manager at Trojan Heat Treat, a metal-finishing manufacturer. A stocky man sporting a beard and mustache, Stonebraker is a kind soul who felt enough of a kinship with his new town to become the village president. When asked about his affinity for Homer, Stonebraker talks about one of his favorite stories. The Stonebrakers moved from Southfield in the winter of 1998, into the teeth of a snowstorm they'd like to forget. But several years later, Jerry wears a big smile when talking about the man who introduced him to small-town hospitality, Homer style.

"I was out and had this little Toro snow blower and was trying to clear the driveway and it was like three feet [of snow]," Stonebraker remembers, lifting his arm to show the snow's height. "The lady who owns the salon here, she says, 'well, my husband will come over and help you.' I said don't worry about it. Ten minutes later I see this huge tractor, her husband's a farmer, the thing's almost as tall as my garage and he can barely fit in the driveway. He comes in with a blade and does about three passes and my whole driveway is clear. We didn't know anybody, but they came in and helped out. Somebody needs a hand and there's always somebody there. This is a great town. I can't say enough good about the village of Homer. Everyone was good to us when we moved here because you never know when you move to a strange town what it's going to be like."

Jerry Stonebraker's kinship to the small blue-collar town isn't unusual. While the Stonebrakers are unique in that they aren't Homer lifers, once they arrived in town they were immediately accepted as one of Homer's own. They moved into a beautiful brick house just around the corner from downtown's Main Street and quickly became entrenched in the community. They joined an arts committee, and Jerry became part of the local government. Like most small towns in the Midwest, Homer is mostly Republican but the village president is a nonpartisan position. Jerry likes it that way. "I try not to get into politics too much," he says. The mayor doesn't want to talk about politics? Only in Homer. But Jerry and everyone else in town are more than willing to talk your ear off about the local sports scene.

Prior to the Homer baseball phenomenon, the biggest sports story to hit the town was a boy named Greg Barton. Born in 1959, Barton was a three-time Olympian in canoeing, and in 1988 he took home two gold medals in the 1,000-meter kayak singles and the 1,000-meter kayak pairs. Those two golds were sandwiched between a pair of bronze medals in 1984 and 1992. Just past the small green sign that welcomes travelers into Homer, there sits another sign proclaiming the village as "Home to Greg Barton." Considered the most prolific U.S. kayaker of all time, Barton was inducted into the Michigan Sports Hall of Fame in 2007. Though he now lives with his family in Charleston, S.C., where he's the president of Epic Kayaks, a manufacturer of high-performance kayaks and paddles, the Barton name remains a meaningful one in Homer. Barton's parents, Mike and Kathleen, own a commercial hog farm in Homer, and "Barton Farms" is as well known as Cascarelli's Pizza to the townsfolk. It took more than 10 years after Barton won his last medal before the world-class kayaker became the second-biggest sports story in Homer.

Photo by Doug Allen.

Talk of the Town

After spending three seasons as a graduate assistant at Spring Arbor University, Tom Salow took his first head-coaching job in 1992 at Homer High School. Though Homer had enjoyed baseball success in the past — including a run to the 1990 state title game — Tom took over a program that had won just two games the year before he arrived. Tom was teaching business and accounting classes at Homer at the time, so he knew the kids. He also knew that some life had to be injected into the program that saw players tuning their old coach out. The new coach immediately took to the task of instilling the Hank Burbridge system that he soaked up as a player and coach at Spring Arbor. In general terms, this meant hustling like crazy all the time, showing respect for one another, and showing respect for the game of baseball.

"It was neat having my own team," said Tom Salow, who was 26 years old when he took over. "I learned a lot from Hank. I did the same things, the same signs, same plays, and same pickoffs. It was difficult, but the kids seemed to buy into what

I wanted. The couple years before that the kids weren't really into baseball. They were looking for a fresh start."

Burbridge deserves the credit for creating the always-hustling system, but it didn't receive a name until Tom's first year at Homer. One of Tom's players, Jason Wolfe, is the person who should be owed naming rights for the "Seven Factor." One day at practice, Wolfe said, "Coach, you say to play every game like it's the seventh game of the World Series. So let's make it seven seconds." True story. That's how it happened. The "Seven Factor" was born. "It could've been five or eight or 10, but that's how we came up with seven," Tom recalled with a laugh.

The Trojans went 13-9 in Tom's first season, an 11-win improvement from the prior year. The foundation for modern-day Homer baseball was being set. Tom, who has a self-described "Bobby Knight style," was laying the groundwork for discipline and playing the game with intensity that would serve Homer for years to come. In his second year, Homer improved by two more games, finishing 15-8. But the real breakthrough came in 1994, Tom's third year at the helm. Behind an excellent pitcher named Jeremiah Johnson, the Trojans won the conference title with a 12-2 league mark and also got their first taste of some real postseason success. A couple late-inning playoff comebacks gave Homer its first district title in several years and then it beat a solid program, Onsted, to reach the Division 3 quarterfinal round. Though the Trojans bowed out in the quarters, the program was slowly but surely gaining momentum. "That's when things started to roll for us," Tom said. "Every year we were taking steps."

From the time Tom Salow became head coach at Homer until the magical run of his brother about a decade later, the Trojans never finished worse than third in the Big Eight Conference. Tom's fourth year was his best yet, a 14-0 conference mark and 24-2 overall record in 1995. It was Homer's second straight conference title, and play-

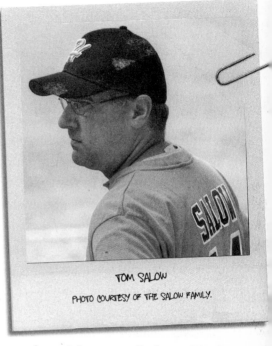

TOM SALOW
PHOTO COURTESY OF THE SALOW FAMILY.

ers understood what playing for a Salow was all about. Tom's hard-nosed style was working, as he played bad cop to younger brother Scott's good cop. After coaching for two years at Taylor Light & Life, a small Christian school on the east side of the state, Scott joined Tom's staff as an assistant in 1996. With Tom coaching third base and Scott at first, the two brothers would look at each other and instantly know what the other was thinking. Whether it was time to bunt or execute a hit-and-run, the two Salows were always on the same wavelength after learning the game's intricacies together in college.

"I remember it being a lot of fun coaching with Tom," Scott said. "We played in so many big games together [at Spring Arbor] that we knew when this situation came up, you do this. We were always on the same page."

Tom, the yeller, was firm and loud at times. Scott, more laid-back, was there to pump confidence back into players after his brother had dressed them down. "I was hard on the guys, especially early on to get things going," Tom said. "I was pretty intense. We didn't like to lose. We just figured, if it was worth doing, than it was worth doing the right way."

At 5-foot-9 and 175 pounds, Scott Salow has a solid, if not imposing, figure. With dark hair and a thin mustache, he has a confident, look-you-in-the-eye demeanor and a warm smile that he regularly flashes. When he's not in shirt-and-tie work attire, Salow can often be found wearing a Homer baseball polo shirt or casual pullover above his jeans or khakis.

Scott is adamant in his belief that Tom set the program in the proper place for the tremendous success that came later. It wasn't just the "Seven Factor," but also a different mentality that was instilled into the program. From the beginning, Tom laid down a rule that players were not permitted to leave town during spring break. What was a standard right of passage among high-school students and baseball players would not be permitted at Homer. Spring break became a time to bond as a team and practice, knowing almost every other team in the state was vacationing that week while the Trojans were getting an edge on the competition. A few players rebelled. A few thought the new regime was loony. Tom didn't care; this was how Homer baseball was going to operate.

"He had the right personality to put those things in place. He had to be tough to tell these kids that we're staying put [during spring break]," Scott said. "He had some very good players that did not play and he had to cut a couple of kids."

Looking back several years now, two games still stick in Scott's mind about his time as Tom's assistant from 1996-2000. The first one was a game at Constantine when the Trojans had the bases loaded and two outs in the late innings of a close contest. Although they usually didn't employ it with two outs, the Salow boys decided to run one of their favorite plays, the catcher pickoff. The play is predicated on the love of catchers to throw runners out on the bases. It usually is run with the bases loaded or runners on first and third. What happens is the batter is told not to swing at a pitch and the runner on first gets a big lead off the bag and then pretends to fall down about 10 feet off first base. As soon as the catcher guns the ball toward first — and he always does — the runner from third sprints home and almost assuredly scores safely. More times than not, the first baseman won't know what to do; he either commits an error or holds onto the ball and lets every runner advance. This time at Constantine, the catcher uncorked the ball into right field, and Homer went on to win thanks to the old "catcher pickoff" play. (That play would later become part of some of Homer's most important moments of state tournament runs and even win the team a few huge games). Scott's second memory is of the one and only time Tom was thrown out of a game. A close play at home plate in a district semifinal game against Tekonsha went against Homer. Tom, being the emotional skip-

SCOTT SALOW
PHOTO BY JOHN GRAP, COURTESY OF THE BATTLE CREEK ENQUIRER

per that he was, raced in to argue the call but before he could get an insult or two in with the home-plate umpire, he was promptly thrown out of the baseball game. "I had to coach the district title game, which we lost to North Adams Jerome, and Tom was out in the center-field bleachers watching," Scott said.

Back then in the early years of the Salow era at Homer, accomplishments like district and conference championships were truly treasured. What later would become just a footnote to bigger things had been a big deal in the late 1990s. There were close games, memorable mob scenes after big wins, and nothing was taken for granted. After leading Homer to a 23-6 record in 2000, Tom Salow decided to step down with a career record of 180-50 (.783 winning percentage). Tom wanted to spend more time with his children, and both Salows agreed it was time for the program to take a different direction. They believed they weren't getting the response from the players they had hoped for and that maybe the players needed a change of scenery. Scott planned on stepping down along with his brother.

At school one day Chuck Finch came down to Scott's classroom. Chuck, who was the junior-varsity coach and the next logical person in line for the varsity job, asked Scott if he really wanted to step down. He said he thought Scott should think it over and keep coaching at Homer. After giving it some time and talking it over with his wife, Scott decided to take the head-coaching job for the 2001 season.

"I really thought Tom would come back at some point," Scott said. "With all the work Tom had put in I just decided I wasn't comfortable with somebody else coaching that third-base box. I expected to hold it for one year while Tom got rejuvenated and was able to refresh himself."

Of course, that never happened. Scott stepped into the head-coaching seat and liked it. Liked it a lot.

>>><<<

While a coaching uncertainty hung over the program at the beginning of 2004, the Homer Trojans squad was shaping up to be a very good team. The year before, Scott Salow ruffled some feathers when he brought up five freshmen to varsity and almost immediately made them starters. This didn't sit real well with the seniors whose spots were being taken. It wasn't a matter of punishing seniors whom Salow wasn't fond of. Instead, the freshmen class of 2003 boasted talent and baseball know-how well beyond their years. With 14-year-old freshmen starting at catcher, third base, shortstop, second base, and center field, Homer went 14-0 in the Big Eight Conference, 30-4 overall and won a district championship. As that was happening, it became harder and harder to disagree with Salow's decision to elevate the young kids up to varsity. Instead of griping about favoritism or anything else, the mantra became, "Wow, we have a chance to be good next year." Heading into 2004, the Trojans weren't just five great sophomores. The soul of the team was a pair of seniors, two great all-around athletes, Josh Collmenter and Matt Powers. Collmenter, a sensational right-handed pitcher, and Powers, a hulking 6-foot-5 first baseman, had welcomed the youngsters with open arms knowing they gave the team the best chance to succeed.

The previous year's 30-win season set a school record and the Trojans were in the midst of six straight 20-win campaigns. As 2004's season began, Homer had big expectations. Winning conference and district titles were no longer the benchmark. These boys wanted to make history. In its best years, Homer had always been stopped in its tracks in the quarterfinal round by a more well-known, perennial-power-type school. Now they wanted to become one of those schools. Leading the charge was Collmenter, a humble but confident player every time he took the field. Next up was Powers, who looked more like major-league first baseman Richie Sexson than a high-school student. Together, the pair was ready to put a bunch of sophomores on their backs and see how far they could go.

On the field, 2004 started just as 2003 left off. Homer was winning and winning big. Perhaps just as importantly, the team was starting to feel an air of invincibility. By mid-spring, the Trojans were 20-0 and beginning to get an inkling that a special season was in their grasp. Around that time, they moved into the No. 1 spot in the state's Division 3 rankings, an honor that certainly took some of the state's powerhouses by surprise. While not exactly a media hotbed yet, the two daily papers that covered Homer, the *Battle Creek Enquirer* and *Jackson Citizen-Patriot*, started to make Homer baseball a regular part of the high-school sports coverage. Television stations from Kalamazoo and Lansing also flocked to town, wondering what was going on in little Homer.

"I remember the point of the season when we were 20-0 and we thought, 'Wow. We've made it this far, why not go all the way?'" catcher Dale Cornstubble said. "Coach always said there's no rule that says we have to lose a game. We took that to heart and had fun doing it." Homer wasn't just winning. It was regularly crushing opponents 15-0 in five innings, throwing no-hitters and hitting grand slams as if that were the norm.

Homer's conference, the Big Eight, is considered a solid small-school baseball league, but it was no match for this special team. Conference foes started considering it a moral victory if the game went all seven innings (high-school games in the state of Michigan are called on account of a mercy rule if a team is up by 15 runs after three innings or 10 runs after five). Practices were more competitive than games, and Salow had to work hard to keep the kids motivated.

For the players, life was status quo on the field and off. The same could not be said for Scott Salow. Months after the emotional board meeting where Salow poured his guts out and community members voiced their opinions before a packed gym, Salow's job status remained in limbo. True, the board had voted unanimously not to accept his middle-school principal resignation, as well as rehiring him as varsity baseball coach. But Chuck Finch wasn't satisfied with that outcome. During the spring of '04, Finch took the next step in what he considered to be "doing the right thing." Finch filed a series of grievances: first orally, then written, and finally in front of the board. Salow did his best to concentrate on baseball but it was difficult. If Salow thought this matter was over with after the emotional board meeting, then that had been wishful thinking. While Finch was the vocal leader of the group that opposed Salow doing both jobs, he wasn't alone in that line of thinking. At the big board meeting back in December of '03, the *Homer Index* quoted two people who spoke at the podium against Salow. One was elementary-school teacher Mary Ann DeGood, who said, "At the risk of being stoned, it is my understanding that when he took the job he was to give his time and heart to the middle-school principal's job. It is unfortunate the superintendent and board didn't close those other doors." Ann Weeks, mother of player Brandon Gibson, said by allowing Salow to do both jobs, it might put the students at risk. "Are we willing to take that risk?" Weeks asked the board, according to the town's weekly newspaper.

After the anonymous letter ripping both Salow brothers circulated around town, the issue became juicy fodder for small-town gossip. Everyone wanted to know, "Who wrote the scathing letter? Would Salow keep both jobs?" Homer's players, who were mostly out of the gossip loop, were even pestered for their thoughts. Mike Warner, veteran publisher of the *Homer*

Index, tried to clear things up when he wrote an editorial in the weekly paper titled, "Anonymous letter well read, not well written." In the editorial's second paragraph, Warner stated his position on the controversy: "As is the case with many unsigned documents, this one was well read but was full of errors and outlandish and exaggerated claims." After disputing the letter's claim that Tom Salow was a poor choice for the high-school-principal job, Warner moved on to the topic of Scott Salow. "The letter said Salow was the least qualified of the four finalists (for middle-school principal) and the district was engaged in 'cronyism' by hiring the younger Salow," Warner wrote. "Contrary to what the letter writers state, Superintendent Brent Holcomb did not select Scott Salow, a search committee did, and it was a unanimous choice.... The real question is who is the person or persons behind this letter. The reaction we've heard from citizens has unanimously been critical of the letter. Residents are more concerned about the writers' identities than the issues raised. Making unsubstantiated charges and hiding behind anonymity is cowardly. Everyone is entitled to their opinion but if you aren't willing to stand up and be counted then you should sit down and shut up."

Warner wasn't the only one publicly endorsing the Salow brothers. In a letter to the editor published by the *Index*, former baseball player Derek Sherman spoke his piece in a note titled, "Homer resident says anonymous letter writers badly miss mark." Sherman writes: "The comments made in the letter were extremely offensive to the school administration and anyone who knows these men personally. The idea of the 'Buddy

System,' which the letter talks about, is ridiculous....No matter what the feeling is, these are two men who have shown they are premier for the job. These men have shown these qualities through their families, their contributions to the community as well as the school, their hard-working attitudes, and their wish for bettering Homer Community Schools." After a few more heated remarks, Sherman signs off with "A person not afraid to leave his name, Derek S. Sherman."

As a tension cloud hung over the small village, the Salow family was hurting. What for most people was intriguing conversation became a real-life soap opera for them. Salow didn't get into coaching for headlines or awards and he certainly didn't seek controversy. Some guilt set in for Salow as he wondered at night what he'd gotten his family and school into. Mostly he kept his thoughts to himself, but Scott's wife was a little more willing to share her feelings.

"I said you don't know the hell we've gone through," Cammy said to anyone who would listen. "These [baseball players] are like our family. He treats these kids like they're his own. This is his life, he's done it forever." Scott, for his part, wished the whole fiasco had never started. He figured Chuck Finch was looking for short-term glory as opposed to the program's stability. Sure, Finch had coached many of Homer's players in summer teams over the years, but why was he pushing this so far? Wasn't it enough to simply watch your son be part of a great team from the stands? Most parents would love that chance. But not Finch. He wanted more.

"I think he had some support verbally," Salow said. "But I think it's because they know what power he maybe has. I don't know how true the support is. I think people will come up to his face, 'Chuck, you've got to go get that baseball job.' Then they'll come to me and say the same thing. But he carries a lot of weight. He was union president, coached a ton of sports. People don't screw with him because he'll come back and bite you in some fashion. There are a lot of things that have happened from his end of it that have been very dirty. He's Jekyll and Hyde. He'll blow by me in the hall one day and not say a word and the next day it's buddy-buddy. I don't know what to expect."

Down at Gale's Barber Shop on Main Street, not a day went by without discussing the Salow situation. Everybody knows Finch, who was born and raised in Homer. Everyone knows the baseball program Salow had put together, and they liked it. Gale Smith has worked at the barbershop since 1968 and owned it since '73. Haircuts cost $10, the shop is closed on Mondays, and Gale's has only one barber chair while about six puffy black chairs line the wall if you'd like to sit down and chat. In an era trending toward smoking bans in bars and restaurants in various cities and entire states, that law is as far from Gale's as the big-city skyline.

A good-looking man with salt and pepper hair, Gale takes a drag off his cigarette while gathering his next thought. With a white shirt, necktie, and khakis, Gale looks professional and smiles kindly. He says about 20 different people are regulars in the shop. One of his favorite sayings is, "Coffee is like advice, it's free." Gale says it's not uncommon to go through five or six pots a day. The shop is a glimpse of the old days, when life was simpler and you met your friends down at the barbershop every day to discuss sports, politics, town events, or whatever else floated your boat.

"I try to make it fun," Gale says. "You can give a guy the worst haircut in the world but if you talk him through it, it'll be OK. I don't get into too much politics or religion. Mostly sports or, now, the economy." Chuck Finch doesn't get his haircuts at Gale's, but the shop owner says they talk "all the time." Gale is a baseball fan too, so he, like everyone else in town, felt immersed in the goings on with Salow, Finch, and the baseball program.

"Chuck is a different type of person because he doesn't mind yelling," Gale said. "But he does it because he cares. You know where he stands. The board was worried about what happens at 3 p.m. when a parent comes to talk to Salow but he's got baseball practice." Everyone had an opinion, and most of them were voiced down at Gale's. Have a smoke and drink some coffee if you'd like.

After clinching the 2004 semifinal win over Muskegon Oakridge, Josh Collmenter pumps his fist in victory.

Photo by Doug Allen, courtesy of the Battle Creek Enquirer.

Seeking a Perfect Season

Homer coasted into the playoffs in 2004 with a perfect 31-0 record and bursting with the confidence that accompanies that kind of mark. They weren't just 31-0. They were 31-0 with almost all shutouts — and victories were usually by scores of 10-0 or 15-0. If there was an unspoken concern among the coaching staff as the playoffs approached, it was because the Trojans hadn't been challenged. How would they respond in a close, late-inning game against a team with similar talent in the state playoffs? In the opening round of districts, Homer won its first two games by a combined score of 17-0. If the games weren't all that exciting, the first of many records to come was pretty neat: After 33 games, Homer set a state record with its 17th and 18th shutouts of the season. Naturally, the road was going to get tougher. But until that happened, Homer was having a good time winning big.

With 33 wins and no losses under its belt, Homer had a full week to prepare for the Division 3 regionals at Springport High School, near Homer. More blowouts were expected as a big crowd gathered on an overcast Saturday afternoon to see what this Homer baseball team was all about. The Trojans easily dispatched Hillsdale 12-1 in the regional semifinal, setting the stage for a regional championship against Manchester High School. During the regular season and early postseason run, Homer's senior star Josh Collmenter was quietly putting together a season for the ages. Everything came together for Collmenter against Manchester, and it was apparent from the early going that something special was taking place. The big right-hander had impeccable command — a quick trip to the concession stand might cause a fan to miss three strikeouts. After five innings, Collmenter had a no-hitter. He also struck out each of the first 15 batters he faced. A Manchester groundout to start the sixth ended up being the only non-strikeout on the unbelievable day for Collmenter. A seventh-inning walk ruined the perfect game, too, but Collmenter finished with 20 strikeouts and a no-hitter as Homer cruised to a regional championship with a 9-0 blanking of Manchester. Afterward, Manchester coach Corey Fether talked about being on the other side of a once-in-a-lifetime performance.

"The kid was phenomenal," Fether told the *Jackson Citizen-Patriot*. "The only thing we could hope for was for him to walk some guys and get a little wild, but he wasn't. He was around the plate the entire time. I got to see probably the best pitcher ever in high-school baseball. Anywhere. I've never seen anybody better than that in high-school baseball."

Scott Salow, who was practically accustomed to these types of outings from Collmenter, was equally awed. "He just doesn't give up runs," Salow said. "He's just unbelievable. It was a game for the ages. To throw a game like that in the regional final against a top-10 team, you don't draw that one up to start the day. You know Josh is going to give you a good outing, hope to keep them to two or three runs, and hope the offense will score. But to do what he did and strike out 20 out of 21 and just miss a perfect game, what can you say?"

The Manchester game was fun and all, but the true test awaited Homer. With just two days of rest, Homer dove into preparing for one of the state's all-time winningest programs, the Blissfield Royals. Led by veteran coach Larry Tuttle, the Royals had seven state championships in their school's trophy case. That was seven more than Homer. The aura of Tuttle and Blissfield was usually enough to intimidate opponents into thinking they were only at the park to play the role of Washington Generals to Tuttle's Globetrotters. Salow was determined not to let his team be intimidated. He only had two days to convince his 35-0 team that Blissfield was just another baseball team; not some unbeatable legion of titans. It was no easy task. An epic match-up was 48 hours away in Howell. Homer vs. Blissfield in the Division 3 quarterfinals. The winner would stamp a ticket to Battle Creek and the state semifinals later in the week.

Practice was upbeat and fairly status quo as Homer's players prepared for the biggest game of their lives. As a big hockey fan, Salow decided to borrow from 1980 U.S. Olympic Team coach Herb Brooks for some advice on readying for a big game as an underdog. Brooks, the leader of the famed "Miracle on Ice" group, tried to make the powerful Russian team look human, like just another hockey team that the Americans had to defeat. That's similar to how Salow went about telling his team what to expect from Blissfield. They were an excellent team, of course, but they were just a high-school baseball team. Salow wasn't bringing Homer to face the New York Yankees in the Bronx.

At 35-0, Homer knew what kind of team it was. However, in their recent history, the Trojans had made it this far a few different times only to be kicked around in the quarterfinals by teams with Blissfield-like pedigrees. On the other side, Blissfield brought a 31-11 record into the game, along with a much tougher regular-season schedule and the confidence that comes with seeing seven state title trophies in your school's hallway. On the Monday night before the big game, Salow traveled to Blissfield High School of all places, for the Division 3 All-Region meeting. Located in the bottom southeast corner of the state, Blissfield is about 30 miles from Toledo, Ohio, and also very close to Monroe — Salow's hometown. Growing up, Salow was well versed on Blissfield and its unrivaled baseball tradition. His father, Tom Salow Sr., was born and raised in Blissfield, back in the day when the school was nicknamed the "Sugarboys," a play on words for the sugar factory in town (they became the Royals in 1958). Scott's brother, Tom Jr., played for Tuttle on an American Legion team several years back. So Scott knew the history, knew what he faced. When he arrived at Blissfield on this day to help decide the All-Region team, Tuttle immediately went into his psychological tactics. Homer's Collmenter and

Blissfield's Ryan Terry had split the votes, 2-2, for who would be the No. 1 pitcher on the All-Region team.

Showing off a couple championship rings on his finger, Tuttle turned to Salow and said, "Here's how we'll break the tie. Whoever wins tomorrow's game, they'll be ranked first." Bring it on, Salow thought to himself.

Earlier in the year, the 60-year-old Tuttle became the winningest baseball coach in Michigan history, passing Grand Ledge legend Pat O'Keefe. In 37 years at Blissfield, Tuttle had amassed almost 900 victories. He stopped teaching at Blissfield in 1999 and began spending winters in Naples, Fla., but every spring he returned to coach the Royals' baseball team. Tuttle's house was across the street from the school, but really, his home was on the ballfield.

Blissfield's baseball facility is ridiculous; think Texas high-school football crazy. That's thanks mostly to a $375,000 donation in 1995 by O.W. Farver, owner of Blissfield Manufacturing, an automotive component supplier and the town's largest employer. All that cash helped produce a field featuring a $17,000 irrigation system with a 50-head underground sprinkler system, sunken Major League-style dugouts, 250 stadium seats behind home plate, and a scoreboard bigger than some backstops. But Blissfield is not just a baseball team, it's also a grassroots program. Part of the massive donation from Farver went toward renovating Little League fields, including an exact replica of Howard J. Lamade Stadium in Williamsport, Pa., where the Little League World Series is played every August. Tuttle had been involved in countless big games and had a few butt-whippings of Homer on his resume. Perhaps that's why the day before the 2004 quarterfinal contest Tuttle told the *Battle Creek Enquirer* that Blissfield had "faced about six pitchers as good as Josh Collmenter this season." Tuttle went on to say, "They haven't seen anyone as good as Terry. I think we have a kid [Terry] who's every bit as good as [Collmenter], if not better."

BRANDON GIBSON LEAPS FOR THE BALL IN RIGHT FIELD.
PHOTO BY DOUG ALLEN, COURTESY OF THE BATTLE CREEK ENQUIRER

As Homer's yellow school bus departed the school parking lot, bound 85 miles northeast for Howell High, Salow had something to show his star pitcher, Collmenter, who was seated near the back of the bus. Trash-talking through the media is usually reserved for professional sports or possibly NCAA Division 1 basketball or football, but now it made its way to Division 3 high-school baseball in Michigan. Salow sauntered toward the back of the bus and handed Collmenter that day's Battle Creek paper, the one where Tuttle basically called Collmenter a dime-a-dozen pitcher. If any motivation had been lacking, and it hadn't, now Homer and especially Collmenter were pumped. They couldn't wait for the bus to roll into Howell. "I just remember we showed up and our side was packed [with fans]," Collmenter said. "And [Blissfield] had just one small section of bleachers filled."

Generally, before a game, Salow let his starting pitcher and catcher work in the bullpen by themselves without being bothered. But on this day, Salow took a long walk out to see Collmenter and gauge how his 15-0 pitcher was feeling before the biggest game of both of their lives. The moment Salow reached Collmenter and looked in his eyes, a sense of relief came over the coach. Collmenter didn't even have to say anything but simply seeing his determined gaze let Salow know his right-hander was going to be just fine. Still, Salow decided to lighten the mood as the first pitch approached. "Josh, you've had a great career and it's great to have you on the mound today, and Coach Tuttle thinks you're one of the six or seven best pitchers he's seen this year," Salow laughed.

On a gorgeous June day, two fantastic high-school baseball teams gave everything they had. The cliché "no one deserves to lose this game" certainly applied. Unfortunately, that's not how sports works. In Homer's half of the second inning, Dale Cornstubble doubled off Terry. With two outs, ninth hitter Brandon Gibson lined a single to center field, scoring Brock Winchell, who was running for Cornstubble, and the Trojans held a precious 1-0 lead. Collmenter, who entered the game with a 0.16 ERA, wouldn't budge. Blissfield's talented leadoff hitter Justin Wilson doubled in the third inning but was stranded. The Royals also induced a few walks, only to be stranded on base as if Collmenter were generously allowing them to get their hopes up. As Salow trotted out to coach third base in the first few innings, he gave himself reassurances, saying to himself, "We're OK. We've held them scoreless for at least a few innings."

On the other side, Blissfield's Terry was nearly Collmenter's match. After the second-inning run, Terry was sharp as he gave up just two more hits while striking out 12. As Homer's orange-clad crowd roared with excitement and nervousness, the Trojans ran out (in seven seconds or less) onto the field in the top of the seventh, still clinging to a perilous 1-0 advantage. Perhaps letting some uncharacteristic nerves sink in, Homer shortstop Ryan Thurston committed an error, allowing the leadoff batter to reach base in the seventh. The next batter popped up a bunt, causing Tuttle to bow his head in anger at the third-base coaching box because, like Homer, Blissfield also reveled in small ball. Then with one out and a runner on first, a tailor-made double-play ball came to third baseman Dusty Compton. Compton threw to second, but second baseman C.J. Finch bobbled the throw and everyone was safe. As tension griped the Homer stands, Collmenter collected his 13th strikeout of the game. Two outs, two on. Next, Collmenter walked his fourth batter of the game, very unusual for a pitcher with control like his. The stage was set. Homer led 1-0 but was in trouble for the first time all day and, frankly, all year. Mounting its first rally of the game, Blissfield had the bases loaded with two outs and, naturally as the baseball gods work,

Justin Wilson, the only Blissfield batter with a hit on the day, at the plate.

Salow took a slow walk out to the mound to address his shaken club. But before he could talk, Finch had run in from second base saying to Collmenter, "My bad, my bad." While Collmenter tried to calm Finch down, Salow looked his players in the eyes and delivered a speech that should be permanently stored in every coach's handbook.

"Man, it doesn't get any better than this. This is great. State quarterfinals, we have a 1-0 game against Blissfield, the defending state champs. This is great and all we need is one more out. This is crazy." As Homer's players regained the swagger they'd displayed for the past 35 games, Salow had one last comment. "I looked at C.J. and said, 'You're going to get the last ball.'"

With that, Salow walked back to the dugout and paced like he never paced before. Wilson, Blissfield's left-handed hitter, dug into the batter's box. A single would likely score two and, with the way Terry was shutting down Homer's hitters, that's probably all Blissfield needed. Since the bases were loaded, Collmenter worked from the windup, not concerned with the lead being taken by any of Blissfield's baserunners. This was a 1-on-1 match now. Collmenter vs. Wilson. As an undefeated season hung in the balance, Wilson rolled over a ground ball to second, right at Finch. Time seemed to stand still as the cherub-faced sophomore Finch picked it up clean and tossed a perfect throw to first baseman Matt Powers. Homer had done it. A massive celebration ensued at the pitcher's mound and it was hard to spot individuals; instead it looked like one big orange glob of humanity. A team. Homer's team.

>>><<<

Two days after striking out 20 batters in a regional championship game against Manchester, Collmenter fanned 13 and allowed just one hit in a magical 1-0 victory over Blissfield. With bedlam ensuing among Homer's fans, Collmenter talked about his performance. "I heard about it on the bus and I thought, 'That was the wrong comment to make,'" he said of Tuttle's remarks. "I knew that would fire us up and get us ready to play. Everybody talks about Blissfield, but I knew we were just as good. We went into it thinking we don't have to beat Blissfield; they have to beat us."

For the first time in 14 years, Homer had advanced past the quarterfinal round. For all the doubters who spoke about a supposed weak schedule, the Trojans had triumphed over the state's most legendary baseball program. "I told the guys, 'We don't have to beat seven state titles. We just have to be one run better,'" Salow said. C.J. Finch said he'd never been more nervous than before that final out was made. "I was trying to calm myself down, not even calm [Collmenter] down," Finch said of the meeting before the last out. "I'm always the kind of player, any ball hit, I want it coming to me. I threw the ball to Powers after I fielded it, just hoping that the throw would be on the money, and it was. That put us on a whole separate page getting past the quarterfinal. That was a big thing to the town of Homer, getting past Blissfield and the quarterfinal."

Sophomore Dan Holcomb added: "Everybody in the state thought, 'You're going up against Blissfield, you've had a great season but you guys can't beat Blissfield.' We knew they were kind of the benchmark for everybody in the state but especially Division 3. That was what coach really played up. Nobody thinks you can do it. Everybody was talking about Ryan Terry but nobody was talking about Josh Collmenter. That was the game that Josh came out and showed everybody, 'I'm Josh Collmenter and we're Homer and we're actually a good team and we can hang with everybody in the state.'" Like most coaches who aren't used to losing, Larry Tuttle was in a grumpy mood after seeing his season end. Still, Tuttle gave props to Collmenter even if he didn't renege on his pregame assessment. "He's a great pitcher and he just threw a better ballgame than what we got," Tuttle said. "The reason we didn't get timely hits was because of him. He ranks up there with the best we've seen this year."

Two games remained for a state championship and undefeated season. Next up for 36-0 Homer was a date with Muskegon Oakridge at Bailey Park in Battle Creek. The winner would play for a Division 3 state title the following day.

If their team is lucky enough to qualify for the state semifinals, Michigan baseball coaches are forced to make a difficult decision on Semifinal Friday unlike any they encounter all year. To avoid destroying the arms of high-school kids, the Michigan High School Athletic Association has a rule that states a player is permitted to throw no more than 10 innings over a two-day period before taking a mandatory 48-hour rest. With semifinals on Friday and finals on Saturday, coaches are faced with a tricky quandary. Throw your ace in the semis and be forced to use lesser arms in the title game? Or save your ace for Saturday and risk not reaching the championship all together? As they got ready for Muskegon Oakridge, the Trojans were in a better position than most pitching-wise. Collmenter was the unquestioned ace, what with his record-shattering numbers and mind-numbing consistency all year. But Salow also had a pair of talented sophomores in his back pocket, Dusty Compton and Dan Holcomb, and they too had put together terrific years while carrying unblemished records.

Partly because he was confident they could beat Oakridge without Collmenter pitching and partly because he needed his ace in the championship game, Salow decided to start the hard-throwing Compton. A bundle of talent wrapped in his 5-foot-7 frame, Compton also had a nice breaking ball to compliment his heater, and he'd shown excellent mound poise all year. Using the opposite theory, Oakridge countered with its senior ace, left-hander Bud Giddings. Utilizing a slow, looping curve ball, Giddings had Homer off balance all day. The Trojans took a 2-0 lead in the third inning but by the fourth, Oakridge had tied the score at 2-2 and had runners on first and second with two outs. Feeling it was now or never, Salow lifted Compton and replaced him with Collmenter. The brilliant ace quickly got out of the jam and the score remained 2-2. By the seventh inning it was still that way.

For the state championships in Battle Creek, both baseball and softball games are played all day Friday and Saturday in the Bailey Park complex. The baseball title games are all at C.O. Brown Stadium in the complex, a 5,000-seat stadium that housed a Midwest League affiliate for 12 years. But half the semifinal games, including Homer-Oakridge,

A CLOSE GAME, AND CONCERN IN THE DUGOUT.
PHOTO COURTESY OF MHSAA.

are played on fields outside the stadium on nice, well-groomed surfaces but without the big seating capacity of C.O. Brown. Fans packed the fence that outlined the field and there wasn't an inch to spare. As the game remained tied into the late innings, the anxious crowd moaned and groaned with each pitch.

Much like his speech in the waning moments of the Bliss-field game, Salow told his players to enjoy the moment. "I told the guys to look around and soak it up," Salow said. "That was the first time I allowed myself to think about that stuff. I said look at this, 'Someone is going to be a hero.' Look at this, it's crazy. We just need one run. Because of the way the bleachers were there [small and close to the field], it was an intimidating crowd." In the top half of the seventh inning, Homer mounted a rally against Giddings. An infield single by Holcomb loaded the bases with two outs. What happened next will go down in Homer history somewhere near the top of a pantheon of highlights. Knowing his team was struggling against the crafty Giddings, Salow decided it was time for the old "runner fall-down play."

As Dale Cornstubble settled into the batter's box, Holcomb wandered way off first base and fell down. Confused, Giddings threw to first to pick off Holcomb. It's exactly what Homer wanted him to do. As soon as Giddings heaved the ball toward first, Homer's Brock Winchell, who was pinch running for Collmenter, sprinted home for the go-ahead run. Oakridge first baseman Derik Morehouse saw what was happening and fired home to catcher Nate Stephenson. The throw actually beat Winchell home but when Stephenson mishandled it, Winchell slid home and the Trojans had a 3-2 lead. Homer's giddy crowd erupted. Yet another foe had been duped by a play Trojan fans had seen oh-so-many times. High-school baseball substitution rules allow a player to re-enter a game if he's been removed for pinch-running purposes, so Collmenter returned to the mound and retired the side in the bottom of the seventh. The Trojans had climbed to 37-0 and were one win away from their first-ever state championship.

"We practice that all the time, probably at least once a practice," Collmenter said of the play. "In fact, we were just working on it yesterday because in the state finals, you figure you're going to need to steal a run or two."

Salow, who was pushing all the right buttons, said the play was done out of necessity. "I felt like we needed to do something to put the ball in motion because we were not hitting.

Everything I heard about [Giddings] was exactly right. Everyone told me I would sit in the dugout and wonder why we couldn't hit him. And that's what I did." Though the Trojans collected just five hits off Giddings, their defense was flawless while Oakridge committed four errors. After blowing out almost every opponent all season, Homer had won two straight one-run games without flinching. As for the pitching situation, since Collmenter threw 3⅔ innings, he'd only be allowed to go 6⅓ on Saturday. Salow wasn't too concerned. That was a problem to worry about tomorrow. "The plan was for Dusty to throw four innings and see where we were. But there was no sense saving Josh."

Collmenter retired the last 11 batters of the game, allowing just one hit and striking out four. He required only 43 pitches to make sure his team would be playing on the last possible day of the 2004 high school season. There was no doubt who'd be taking the ball in the state championship the next afternoon. Josh Collmenter had pitched too many innings, collected too many records, and led a sophomore-laden team too far to see somebody else control the outcome of his senior season. Tired arm be damned.

As an undefeated small-town phenomenon, Homer entered the state finals weekend as the biggest story in Battle Creek. Now, as word spread over the base-running ingenuity that won the semifinal game, the Trojans' state title game became a must-watch event. Reporters from Detroit to Grand Rapids to Flint crowded the press box high above home plate on Saturday afternoon to see if history would be made. After

Friday's victory, the Michigan High School Athletic Association revealed that no team in the 34-year history of the state tournament had ever completed an unbeaten season. Homer was one game from rewriting that history.

With the bull's-eye squarely on the backs of its orange T-shirts (they called them jerseys) Homer had marched, or occasionally tiptoed, through the state tournament. Two straight last-inning victories proved this wasn't just a team that beat up on small-school nobodies all year. This was a confident, talented outfit with one last thing to prove.

The entire town of Homer — literally — excitedly packed into C.O. Brown Stadium for one last emotional ride with their boys. Win or lose, this would be the last high-school game for Collmenter and Matt Powers, the first baseman who set a single-season school record with 15 home runs. Over half the starting lineup were sophomores, but this would be it for Collmenter and Powers. Homer's fans in orange filled C.O. Brown, a sight virtually never seen for the Midwest League team that played 70 dates there every summer. The MHSAA doesn't gather attendance numbers for state finals games because fans can buy tickets for one game or all-day passes, so therefore it's impossible to know exactly how many people are at one particular game. But the MHSAA did estimate that more than 3,000 were at Homer's state final, a simple conclusion because the entire grandstand was filled with orange. John Johnson, the MHSAA's director of communications, said he'd never seen a crowd like that for Michigan's baseball finals. The only Homer residents not at the game were either too ill to attend or simply didn't have a pulse.

Despite throwing about 100 innings during the season, including 3⅔ the day before, Collmenter was his usual self against Shepherd High in the final. Before the game, Salow pondered what to do about getting two outs from someone not named Collmenter. The ace only was allowed 6⅓ innings so somebody else had to contribute. Since Salow didn't want one of his sophomores entering a late-inning pressure situation, he used Compton to get the final out of the second inning and the first out of the third. Under high-school rules, a pitcher can leave the game and re-enter at any point later in the same game.

"I went out there to make the change and the crowd was going, 'Hey, what's going on?'" Salow said. Compton got both outs without a problem, and now the game was back in Collmenter's hands. Without fail, this was always a good approach for Homer. Facing Shepherd pitcher Alex Dawe, who entered the game 14-0 on the year, the Trojans scored once in the second and twice more in the third. By that time, the inevitable had sunk into the packed house of Homer fans. Collmenter wasn't going to give up three runs. Hell, he entered the game with *two* earned runs allowed all year. Shepherd tacked on one unearned tally in the sixth, but that was all they'd get. Perhaps unnerved by the stage and the opponent, Shepherd committed six errors in a game where it needed to be perfect.

As Collmenter trotted out to the mound in the seventh inning protecting a 5-1 advantage, he paused and looked all around him. "That's the first time I really soaked it all in," Collmenter said. "I stepped in back of the mound and scanned the crowd, behind home plate all the way down the side, and it's just packed in orange and black. You just get goose bumps seeing everyone and they're standing on their feet and cheering for you and for the town. When you're from a small town, people think we can't be any good. But our hometown faithful knew how we could play and they kind of had the same attitude that we did. That we're going to play anybody and we can beat anybody."

Collmenter gave up three hits and struck out 11. With the crowd on its feet and roaring, Shepherd's Jamie Wilmot hit a bouncer back to Collmenter with two outs in the seventh. Collmenter calmly fielded the ball and flipped over to fellow senior Powers. That was it. Homer won 5-1, finishing the year 38-0 to become the first Michigan team to complete a season undefeated since the 1971 inception of the state tournament.

"It's a dream come true," said Powers, a 6-foot-5 gentle giant who finished the season with 73 RBI. "The way we've done it and to go undefeated all year is just great. I love it."

The storybook season even had a fitting ending when Collmenter and Powers, the two seniors, combined for the historic final out. "That play couldn't have been drawn up any better," Salow said. "Those two deserved to have their hands on the last play."

Collmenter ended his senior season without a Division 1 scholarship offer, yet with numbers you have to look at twice to believe. And then you'll think they were incorrectly typed:

18-0 record, 0.13 ERA, two earned runs allowed in 105 ⅔ innings, 223 strikeouts, and 23 walks.

While all of Homer posed for pictures with the players and gathered for what amounted to a town celebration in the outfield of C.O. Brown Stadium, Coach Salow had a phone call to make. Only moments after the best athletic achievement of his life, Salow's mind drifted elsewhere. As his players rejoiced with family and friends over their 38-0 masterpiece, Salow grabbed his cell phone and from the outfield grass placed a call to his mentor, Hank Burbridge, who was dying of cancer in Spring Arbor, 40 miles from Battle Creek. Burbridge would assuredly have been at the game if his health allowed. But in recent months the cancer had taken over his body, and he rarely left the bedroom. For Salow, despite the ecstasy of the moment, he wished the man who taught him so much about baseball could have been there to see it.

"I was standing right next to the bed and there were tears on both ends," said Pat Burbridge, Hank's wife. "I think he felt the pride of a father and a son. He always called him Scotty. He welcomed him to Championship Land. Scott and Tom were both recruited by Hank. My husband had an uncanny way of seeing peoples' character. He could feel something about a young man. He saw such stability in these boys. There was such a foundation in Scott and Tom. [Hank] thought Scott had the tenacity and courage to coach kids. These young men that went into coaching were just like his sons. He felt a kinship with these kids." Although Burbridge died less than a year later in February 2005, he had long before helped turn a young man from Monroe into a championship-level coach.

Photo by Doug Allen.

Mentoring Excellence

Scott Salow was a decent high-school baseball player at Monroe High, but he wasn't fighting off scouts and college recruiters upon graduation in the spring of 1987. Scott's older brother Tom, on the other hand, had been an excellent high-school player and continued to the next level for the NAIA's Spring Arbor College. When Scott showed an interest in joining Tom at the small Christian college, coach Hank Burbridge didn't mind taking in the smallish brother of his starting first baseman. For Scott, getting a chance to play for any college team — let alone one with his brother — was a thrill. Adding to his excitement was Spring Arbor's high-ranking status among NAIA schools. Burbridge was a small-school legend and a fixture at Spring Arbor since 1964. When Scott arrived at Spring Arbor in '88, Burbridge had put together 24 consecutive winning seasons. The streak would reach 34 before it ended. As a freshman, Scott was thrust into the starting line-up when the regular shortstop got hurt about halfway through the season.

LONGTIME SPRING ARBOR COACH HANK BURBRIDGE.

PHOTO COURTESY OF SPRING ARBOR UNIVERSITY.

"I'd go in at short-stop," Scott remembers. "I was an average high-school player; the only reason he put me on the team was because of my brother. That experiment [of starting] lasted maybe a week. Then he moves me to second, which was my high-school position. I had maybe 80 at-bats that year and I didn't play in the postseason." Sophomore year, Scott got about 80 more at bats, hitting a robust .170. Apparently, Burbridge was looking for a little more oomph out of his second baseman. By the time Scott's junior year rolled around, he was way back on the depth chart. We're talking *way* back.

"I was thinking I'd get a shot to play but there were at least eight and maybe 10 or 12 second basemen that year," Scott said. "That year he brought in a great player, a kid from Canada who was a non-traditional student and was 28 years old. I batted four times that year, 0-for-4. I think he forgot I was on the team."

By then, Scott was more of a coach than a player. He might've been listed as a junior infielder on the roster but he was really an assistant coach. His duties ranged from coaching first base to pitching batting practice to hitting infield/outfield balls. "And I loved it," he said, "so I think when games got out of hand, he forgot to put me in."

When Spring Arbor was in the field, Scott was next to his coach, soaking up all he could from the man who would eventually win 1,000 baseball games. He'd long since given up on his playing career, instead focusing on the future and how he could stay in the game. As Scott's senior year wound down, the Spring Arbor Cougars got hot and reached the NAIA World Series in Lewiston, Idaho. Spring Arbor lost the first game of the double-elimination tournament with its ace on the mound, and its chances for bringing a championship back to Michigan were slim. Scott glanced at the lineup card as the Cougars warmed up for their second game. He couldn't believe what he was reading. For some reason, Burbridge penciled him in as the designated hitter, batting eighth. "I'm terrible, maybe he thought I was going to jumpstart the lineup or something," Scott said. "The sad thing is, I'd like to know who I DH'd for. They've got to be feeling bad. I went 1-for-4 with a single. I think [Burbridge's] point was, 'I haven't forgotten about ya.' Otherwise why would he have put me in? Why now? We're in the World Series." Spring Arbor lost the game, and Scott had a long plane ride home to think about his future in baseball and why on earth he was in the lineup that day.

Years later, Tom Salow says he's not surprised that his brother became a stellar coach. "He took it all in, absorbed it all," Tom says. "There was no doubt he'd be very successful when he got his own team. He really works at it and prepares. He's always on top of game situations when they come up; always thinking ahead of the game." Burbridge, who is a member of five halls of fame, schooled the Salow boys on more than just hustling onto the field and how to bunt. "He taught us so much about baseball, life, and work ethic," Tom said. "About not wasting days of our life and putting things in perspective. The sun will always come up the next day. We've tried to do those things at Homer." While Scott Salow borrowed a ton from Burbridge's baseball glossary, he did deviate on some other things. "I think I coach like him except that Coach Burbridge, like my brother, forgot about the guys on the bench," Scott said. "And once he had his lineup, it's set. I do that too, but I try hard and I'm intentional with making sure all the kids feel good about themselves, that everyone gets the same amount of batting practice. Under Tom, guys would get one at-bat a year, and Coach Burbridge too. Maybe because I sat on the bench, I know how that feels."

More than a decade after Salow's unspectacular college career, he couldn't figure out why the best player he'd ever been around wasn't attracting more collegiate suitors. Josh Collmenter got called up to Homer's varsity team during his freshman season. A bespectacled, nerdy-looking sort, Collmenter displayed poise and mound presence well beyond his years. A gifted athlete who also excelled in basketball, Collmenter grew and grew, eventually reaching 6-foot-3 and 230 pounds as a senior, shedding the glasses along the way. His physical growth only helped on the baseball field where he began adding a crisp fastball to his unshakable makeup.

Yet halfway through his senior season, Collmenter was still looking for a Division 1 scholarship offer. Even though two-hit shutouts with 12 strikeouts became the norm, Collmenter had a better chance at hailing a cab in Homer than getting a sit-down conversation with a Division 1 coach. His grades? 4.0. Social problems? Not even close. He was probably the most well-liked kid in town, being as courteous to a school librarian or disabled child as he was to baseball coaches. Salow said Collmenter was akin to a college kid still in high school with the way he performed practical jokes on his teammates. A true character, Collmenter could ease tense situations with his fun-loving demeanor.

JOSH COLLMENTER ON THE MOUND IN PLAYOFF COMPETITION.
PHOTO COURTESY OF MHSAA.

Size? Check there too. Stats? No one in the state could compare. The amazing part is that Collmenter didn't become bitter over the process. Some coaches, teammates and friends did, but that wasn't his way. It would all work out, Collmenter told those who were exasperated over his lack of attention from recruiters. Maybe he was throwing things against his bedroom wall, keeping the anger inside of him while people were present. Nope, that didn't happen either, according to his younger brother, Cody. The even-keeled pitcher was a reflection of his steady persona off the field.

"We didn't have a radar gun or anything so I didn't know how fast I was throwing," Collmenter said. "I knew I was doing well but I didn't know my stats other than what we saw in the *Enquirer* and *Cit-Pat*." (Salow doesn't let the team see their stats during the year because, he reasons, the only thing that matters is wins and losses.) "I didn't want to settle for anything. I left my options open and if it came down to it, I probably was going to go to Kellogg Community College [in Battle Creek]. I'd rather do that and try to move on than settle for Division 3 schools like Hillsdale or Adrian or something like that. You think about the small-school bias a little bit. Obviously, scouts aren't going to come watch a Homer-Athens game over something else. So it was a little bit of, 'You're from a small town.'"

After the Manchester performance when Collmenter struck out 20 of 21 batters, Salow started venting to the press about his star's situation. Whether that had anything to do with it or not, Collmenter went from unknown to sought-after commodity during the Blissfield game. Though he didn't know it at the time, coaches from almost every Division 1 school in the state came to watch how Collmenter would stack up against a powerful team like Tuttle's Royals. Halfway through the game as Collmenter was tossing yet another masterpiece, college coaches got on their cell phones and starting calling their head coach or another assistant to come see this kid from Homer. When it was over and Collmenter led Homer to the 1-0 win, he got his first real taste of being coveted. "I was just trying to get some food after the game and [the college coaches] all wanted to come talk to me," Collmenter said. "I told the pitching coach at Central Michigan that I didn't even realize he was there."

Soon thereafter, Collmenter took recruiting visits to Eastern Michigan and Central Michigan. He had a 48-4 career record and his name was littered all over the state record books. After mulling the decision for a short time, the best pitcher in Homer High School history decided to take his talents to Central Michigan University of the Mid-American Conference in Mount Pleasant.

>>><<<

When Scott Salow raised the championship trophy he worked so hard to achieve, he did so not knowing if he'd coached his last game at Homer. Even though Chuck Finch's efforts to force Salow into a baseball or principal decision were squashed, Finch didn't stop there. Unsatisfied with what he thought was a clear violation of Homer's past precedent, Finch began filing a series of grievances against Salow holding two prominent positions. Salow was convinced the only reason Finch was giving him hell was because he wanted the glory of coaching this great run of Homer talent, including C.J., Chuck's son. Finch didn't see it that way. "I would've loved to coach these kids in high school but not at the extent of undermining Scott," Finch said.

"You might want to look behind that picture and see what was at work the last five years [of coaching]. It was a matter of doing the proper thing as far as past practice."

With one championship in the bag and a class for the ages just coming up on their junior years, Homer should have been living the high life. But it was far from that. A couple uncomfortable months were in store for the reigning Division 3 baseball champs and, more specifically, Coach Salow.

Photo by Doug Allen.

Battle Beyond the Baselines

As summer rolled into fall 2004, Salow had a few more items to place in his memorabilia-filled home office. There were pictures, newspaper articles, and letters of congratulations on the team's stirring state championship run. There were individual awards, as well, including the Division 3 and overall Coach of the Year honors, presented by the Michigan High School Baseball Coaches Association at a banquet in Mount Pleasant. It should've been the perfect icing on the cake for a coach who was beginning to render Homer a renowned baseball commodity.

But there was no post-championship honeymoon period for Salow. It wasn't as if Chuck Finch was hovering over Salow's shoulder during school (the middle school and high school are in the same building), or hiding behind his backyard bushes like in the movies. But Salow felt the heat. During the '04 school year, Finch filed three grievances trying to stop Salow from being both principal and baseball coach. The process started with Finch's verbal grievance. Then he filed another with Superintendent Holcomb and, finally, with the school board at a regularly scheduled meeting. The grievances were all rejected, but Finch, with the backing of the HEA, pursued a final step. An impartial arbitrator would be brought in to decide once and for all if Salow could keep both positions.

Art Welch has spent his entire adult life teaching at Homer, most recently college prep courses in grades 10-12. Welch has served several different positions on the HEA over the years and considers himself a very active union member. Not surprisingly, he was backing Finch on this issue. "The teachers said they thought Scott Salow would be a good principal but they didn't want him to be principal if he continued to coach," Welch said. "When the board [essentially] said we don't care what the teachers want, it created a real block."

Donald Sugerman, a veteran arbitrator from Ann Arbor, would analyze the case. Homer Community Schools selected the Lansing-based Thrun Law Firm, P.C. to represent it and Salow. Kenneth Leche was hired to plead Finch's case by the Michigan Educational Association, the parent organization of the HEA. Instead of soaking in the glow of a state title, Salow was spending time meeting with lawyers and going over details of his professional life. In the case of Homer Education Association (Finch) vs. Homer Community Schools (Salow), Finch was arguing that the teachers' contract was violated when he was not interviewed or hired as the head varsity baseball coach. A hearing took place on Sept. 16, and Michigan's reigning Coach of the Year had no idea if he was going to be out of a baseball job. Both sides would prepare their cases and present them to Sugerman a month later. Sugerman then would have 35 days to decide the fate of two Homer men.

In the legal brief, Finch's side is referred to as the "association," and Salow's representatives are the "district." Also, the term "bargaining unit member" indicates teachers who are members of the HEA. "*The association contends that by 'past practice' an interview and hiring of the most senior bargaining unit member is required when filling coaching positions,*" wrote Joe Mosier, the chief lawyer working the case for Thrun. He continued:

> *However, examples were provided by the District to show that there is no clear past practice of always interviewing and hiring the most senior (HEA) member. In fact, during the 2003-04 school year, over half of the coaching positions in the District were filled with (non-HEA) members. Superintendent Holcomb testified that it is not a rare occurrence in Homer that non-HEA applicants are hired over HEA applicants. Moreover, the District provided a number of unrefuted examples establishing that:*
> » *Extracurricular coaching positions have been filled from outside the (HEA) instead of with (HEA) members.*
> » *Administrators have served as coaches.*
> » *Individuals have been hired without interviews.*
> » *Off-staff certified teachers have been hired for certified bargaining unit positions when on-staff candidates were considered but not given the positions.*

Mosier gave a brief summary of Salow's baseball qualifications, including the undefeated season and state championship to further state his case. Though the baseball results weren't the core of the coach's defense, they were used as evidence that he had full control of those responsibilities.

Even the people expected to aid Finch's case were saying all the wrong things for the grievant. Isabel Nazar, who had been the association president, a member of the Board of Governors and on the association's bargaining teams for 20 years, testified that the so-called "practice" has been "arbitrary, willy-nilly, and has not followed the association's understanding and intent."

At the beginning of Finch's post-hearing brief, Leche explained the collective bargaining agreement between Homer schools and the teachers' union. Concise descriptions of the grievance process are laid out, concluding with "Level Four," where an arbitrator is brought in if the union is not satisfied with the board's decision.

When the Board filled the vacant position of Head Varsity Baseball Coach with a person employed in an administrative capacity (Principal), did the Board violate, misinterpret, or misapply multiple sections of the collective bargaining agreement?

Unequivocally, the answer is yes!

The brief goes on to argue it was unfair that neither Finch nor football coach Rob Heeke, the two people who applied for the temporarily vacant baseball job, were not interviewed. According to the HEA, Homer and its school board were making an egregious mistake in allowing Salow to perform principal and baseball coach duties simultaneously. The HEA's argument relied primarily on a "past practice" that wasn't part of any negotiated contract rules.

In its summary, the HEA stated:

When the board ignores its contractual responsibilities to its employees, it ignores the practice of the parties, ignores giving first consideration to those who own the right to be first considered, the Board may expect to have teachers take exception to such attitudes and behaviors. The process is especially vital when the contractual rights of bargaining unit members are being undermined through an abuse of power rather than by playing by the rules.

Over to the east in Ann Arbor, while arbitrator Sugerman was trying to figure out what the heck was going on in this case of small-town politics in Homer, junior Dan Holcomb also was having a tough time trying to sort things out.

An all-around athlete, Holcomb was quarterbacking the varsity football team that fall. But his mind never strayed far from the baseball field, which was his true love. Holcomb was one of the Fab Five who started as freshmen and then again as sophomores during the 38-0 season. Though he would later become a record-setting pitcher, Holcomb played center field his sophomore season, and did it well. Dan might've preferred

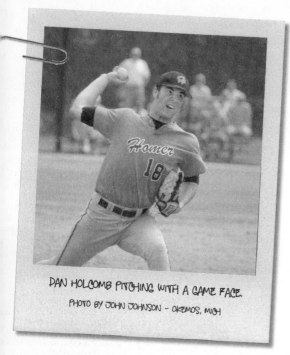

DAN HOLCOMB PITCHING WITH A GAME FACE.
PHOTO BY JOHN JOHNSON - OKEMOS, MICH

to just think about sports all the time, but when your dad is the school's superintendent, it can be a chore to stay out of the political loop.

"My dad didn't talk to me much about it. I know he wanted Coach Salow to remain coach, but it wasn't his decision," Dan said. "In school, you just had to sit back because people said, 'Your dad fired Coach Salow.' People didn't understand it wasn't his decision. It was a really awkward time."

Making things even more uncomfortable was the players' long-term relationship with Finch. All the boys grew up playing sports with C.J., and Chuck was often their coach. They also knew Chuck from school and knew his aggressive nature. Some of them played for him on the junior-varsity football team; still more played for him in youth baseball leagues in Marshall, a nearby town with more people and resources than Homer. No matter where the players went, they were hounded by questions about the baseball situation. They had to take care to remember if they were talking to a friend of Salow's or a confidant of Finch's so they didn't say the wrong thing to the wrong person. It was a lot for 15- and 16-year-olds to endure.

"We all tried to stay out of it because everybody knew Chuck really well," Dan Holcomb said. "We all had him as a teacher. We didn't dislike Chuck or anything, but we all loved Coach Salow and we didn't want to see him lose his job because he got a promotion [to principal]. I don't think there was necessarily bitterness toward Chuck, it's just that people wanted Coach Salow to stay. With C.J., you didn't come out and say we don't want your dad. Coach Finch grew up here so he knows everybody in town. Everybody was just kind of torn. They didn't know what side to go on."

There was one player not the least bit torn on the Salow-Finch debate. Junior Dusty Compton, another of the Fab Five, was the emotional leader of the group and he had a very tight bond with his coach. Compton is a true one-of-a-kind, both on and off the field. On the field, he is a 5-

CHUCK FINCH COACHING AT
A 2000 YOUTH TOURNAMENT IN JAPAN.
PHOTO COURTESY OF THE FINCH FAMILY.

foot-7, Joe Average–looking kid who throws the type of smoke that makes an opponent's eyebrows elevate off his head when standing in the batter's box. He is a gifted baseball player who lives and breathes the game. Dusty might've fit better in a different generation, say the 1950s, where playing pickup baseball from 10 a.m. 'til sunset was a way of life. He would have loved that. Dusty has little interest in other sports and probably even less in academics; Dusty's lone motivation to pass classes was to stay eligible for baseball season in the spring. Asked by a reporter once what his favorite subject was, Dusty looked him in the eye with a grin on his face and said, "gym." Out on the middle of the baseball field, standing atop the mound with everybody in the yard watching him, Dusty was at ease, in his element. He was a pitcher, and that's why he got up in the morning. Like everyone else on the team, Dusty knew Chuck Finch. Perhaps because their personalities didn't mesh, Dusty wasn't a big Finch fan.

"I wouldn't want to play for anybody except Coach Salow," Dusty said in his slow drawl during his junior year. "I wasn't going to play if he wasn't coach. I was going to move to Battle Creek and play for Lakeview [High School, another good baseball school]. Me and Mr. Finch just didn't get along, and I didn't want to play for him at all. It was a real hard time."

No one else on Homer's team lived with a situation like Dusty's. Homer is by no means a wealthy town, but it is a family-oriented place, and most kids have a mom and dad at home or divorced parents that both remain in their lives. Dusty lived in the poor part of town with his mom and older brother. He hardly ever saw his dad, who lived out-of-state, and he wasn't blessed with a nice, stable home life that most of his teammates took for granted when they drove off after practice or a game. Often drifting from one player's house to another, Dusty didn't so much live with his mom as much as he kept his clothes at her residence. A give-you-the-shirt-off-his-back type of kid, Dusty made friends wherever he went, and it wasn't uncommon for him to know a player or two on nearly every opposing team the Trojans played. In the summer, he'd rotate between staying at friends' houses in Battle Creek, Marshall, Homer, and anywhere in between. It was hard to pin down where Dusty might be, but there was a good chance it was on a baseball diamond somewhere. Salow took to calling him "the most misunderstood kid in our school" over the years as teachers and administrators mistook Dusty's academic shortcomings for aloofness or selfishness.

"He'd give you a dollar and he didn't have a dollar," Tom Salow said. "If somebody was going through a difficult time, he'd call them on the phone to see how they were doing. He looked out for others when maybe he should've been looking out for himself. Everybody kind of pulled for Dusty. If you said there's no baseball this year because of budget cuts, Dusty would be out of school. He'd go find baseball somewhere else. He's a pretty smart kid but he did just enough to get by. Dusty was the spirit of our team."

In the winter of 2004, Homer baseball was in jeopardy of losing its spirit as well as its coach.

On November 30, Joe Mosier of Thrun Law Firm sent superintendent Brent Holcomb a fax that was sure to put a smile on the administrator's face. It was Sugerman's denial of Finch's grievance. Mosier wrote: "I am certain that the Board and Administration will be relieved to know that the outcome was favorable for the District." The last line stated that Homer Community Schools District owed Sugerman $1,514.45 — the same amount billed the MEA — for his services. Holcomb and the board were more than happy to pay it.

Under the title "Concluding Findings," Sugerman said the contract does not reserve coaching positions exclusively for unit employees. He said the failure to interview couldn't be used to leverage an employee who was not interviewed for the position. With his unequivocal opinion denying the grievance, Sugerman ended the Homer debate once and for all.

>>><<<

Fourteen months after the whirlwind began, Scott Salow's nightmare was over. A tremendous sigh of relief overcame his body. He hugged his wife and whispered, "It's over." Salow had felt like a prisoner in his own town for the last year. He didn't know how soon life would return to normal but right now, he didn't care. No more grievances. No more worrying at night about what the future held. No more arbitrators dissecting his life's work and asking how much it meant to him.

As happy as Salow was when the arbitration was over, Gary Tompkins might have been able to match his level of relief. Homer's school-board president by day, Tompkins is one of its biggest baseball fans when the final school bell rings and he can loosen his tie. Tompkins was a baseball player at Homer himself, a member of the 1990 team that reached the state finals before losing to Saginaw Nouvel. He understood what baseball meant to his town, and attending the state finals in Battle Creek was a thrill for Tompkins and his young son. "It meant more than words can even describe," Tompkins said of the championship feeling.

"When I equate it to those who say community spirit is dead — well, it's not dead in a small town. When you're able to see 3,000 orange shirts in the crowd … and we got to enjoy the whole moment. I think for us, that tells us what kind of community we are. We're small-town America and we support our kids. It warmed my heart and put a tear in my eye. This is why I live here. This is why my wife and I made the decision to stay here and raise our family here. It's about what you see in the stands."

Tompkins is downright giddy when he describes how proud he was of the team and their championship. The smile is still on his face as he speaks about how the 9- and 10-year-olds in Little League are learning the "seven-second rule," about hustling on and off the field at all times. Unfortunately for Tompkins, other parts of the Homer baseball story weren't as heart-warming. Part of his duties as school board president required him to be involved in the front lines of the Salow-Finch controversy; obviously it was not nearly as joyous as watching high-school baseball alongside his community members.

SCOTT SALOW NEXT TO
A TIGHTLY PACKED HOMER TROPHY CASE.

PHOTO BY DOUG ALLEN.

"That was a difficult time because I know Scott as an instructor and as a teacher here, and I know his passion for baseball. A lot of people didn't know his passion," Tompkins said. "And not only that, but how well he dealt with parents. We couldn't lose by keeping him on as both roles. It made our job very easy when you have 250 people in your board meeting and they're all in support of him. It shows how much our community cares for him."

>>><<<

Meanwhile, on the other side of town, the mood was quite different at the Finch residence.

Have a chat with Chuck Finch and the encounter can go one of two ways. If Chuck is in a good mood, he's a fine fellow to talk with; an intelligent man with good stories to tell. If he's having a bad day, though, abrasive Chuck is enough to make big, strong football players shake with fear. Finch had no problem with discussing his part in the 14-month grievance-turned-arbitration case to remove Salow from the dual positions. Despite what Sugerman ruled and what seemed to be a false (or maybe just vague) rule about not being a coach and administrator, Finch held to his guns even after the fact.

"What happened with that arbitration case is that Homer has always had the policy of not hiring a coach if he is an administrator," Finch said. "There were a lot of shenanigans going on behind the scenes. [Salow] was told he wouldn't have to give up the job. Thirty years of past practice says principals cannot coach. The hiring committee was concerned that academics should be number one. The arbitration wasn't an issue between me and Scott. I warned him before I grieved it that administrators aren't supposed to coach. It's just too big a time commitment to do both jobs well. It wasn't me versus Scott. It was a little uncomfortable. But there are principles to be upheld and that's what I was doing. I like Scott. It was really a union issue. Scott's a good man."

Finch, who has been a high-school social-studies teacher at Homer for more than 20 years, still felt like he was correct in the matter of Salow's two-job role. To this day, Finch claims he was just doing what was right.

"The MEA (Michigan Education Association) didn't argue it well," Finch said. "They didn't bring up past practice. They argued with contract language alone. We didn't do a very good job arguing the case or we would've won. The school wound up winning at the cost of a lot of hard feelings. Unfortunately, it was something that had to happen. I told Scott, 'If I'm not the coach, there's no one else I'd rather have coach than you.'

"Scott lost some credibility," Finch continued. "It's too bad, because, honestly, he should've never been put in that position. They should have been up front with him. It's difficult because peoples' toes have been stepped on. The grievance had to be filed because otherwise you're changing the language of the contract of what's happened over the last 30 years. As a parent, I was concerned. If they hadn't won a state title and achieved maximum success, I would have been one pissed-off dude. I'd have been mad. I put in a lot of time driving over the summer [taking C.J. and his friends to games over the years]. Luckily, things turned out well for them."

One of Finch's stated problems: what happens when Salow's principal duties require him to stay in school past the final bell? With the kids out on the practice field and no coach present, Finch worried that any number of things could go wrong. This, among other things, didn't sit well with Finch.

For Chuck Finch, the matter was much deeper than a grievance or arbitration case. Along with Tom Sharpley in Marshall, Finch had coached C.J. and many of the other Homer boys throughout their youth playing days. Finch felt a kinship and connection to the kids and, naturally, he wanted to coach them in high school, too.

"Nobody ever argued my credentials. That was never an issue," he said. After all the car trips and countless hours spent on practice fields and youth tournaments, Finch wanted to see the process through. Whether he vocalized it or not to the administration, he had no intention of being the high-school coach for the long haul. "Once my kid is done, it doesn't mean two beans to me. I don't need any more placards on the wall."

One of those players who was coached by Finch in pre-high school ball was Dan Holcomb. While Holcomb is quick to praise Salow and loved playing under his varsity coach, he admits that Finch and Sharpley were also influential in his and his teammates' baseball development.

"Definitely Tom Sharpley and Chuck both really helped all of us a lot," Holcomb said. "Especially playing in Marshall, they were the ones who gave us a ride to every game. They were helping us on how to field a groundball, how to field a fly ball and about hitting and pitching. They helped us understand the game of baseball. Growing up playing Homer Little League, it's a lot of fun, but a lot of times it's the dads coaching who have never played baseball before in their lives. Then you go [to Marshall] and it's two guys who know a lot about baseball. With Evan Sharpley and Digger Towe [a future major-league draft pick from nearby Charlotte], there's a lot of baseball that you had to pick up and they helped us learn a lot of what we know now."

Any superintendent of any school district is bound to have difficult moments when politics intervene and you're obligated to pick a side. This was one such time for Brent Holcomb. A former athlete himself, Holcomb is as comfortable talking about a spread offense in football or a hit-and-run in baseball as he is discussing a school bond. At this particular time, Holcomb would've much rather been embroiled in a sporting game. Admittedly, Holcomb respected Salow and loved having a person he regarded of high moral character coaching his son Dan. He had also known Finch for several years, but the two wouldn't be accurately described as close. As the Salow-Finch case wore on, Holcomb second-guessed himself and wondered what he could've done differently. Whichever way the case turned out, clearly it was a black eye for Homer schools to engage in such a messy public dispute.

"I'm disappointed that it happened," Brent Holcomb said. "For me it seemed unnecessary. Scott was clearly the right person and could do both jobs. I can't quibble about the process because the union and Mr. Finch were well within their rights to go down the path that they chose. I understand the concern about having an administrator [also be a] coach. But I also know in a small school district there are limited opportunities to have quality people coaching."

At the time, Homer's players didn't talk about what was going on surrounding their coach. Even after the fact some of them weren't comfortable addressing the situation. But some did, and they mostly spoke about loving to play for Salow.

Shortstop Ryan Thurston: "I was scared that he wasn't going to coach. I had him for the first two years and I wanted him to keep coaching. It would've been really hard to see [a change]. There were quite a few players at the board meeting. I don't think [Finch's] communication skills were good for baseball."

Utility player Brock Winchell, who also played under Finch in football: "Chuck knows his stuff but football is more suited for him. He's a yeller and he'll smack you upside the head. Football is Chuck's game. People were bitter but nobody showed it. I think most of the community wanted Coach Salow to stay."

Years after the case, Brent Holcomb says he doesn't feel like he did anything wrong. Some feelings were hurt, some egos were bruised, but that's what happens when emotions are running at blast-furnace levels about passionate subjects. Chuck Finch's chance to coach a state championship team was over. Finch wasn't going anywhere; you'd have to do a lot more than defeat him in an arbitration case to run Chuck Finch out of his hometown. C.J. Finch and the rest of the Fab Five were juniors now and they had a second consecutive state title in their sights. Scott Salow was sleeping better at night because his job was no longer being bandied about in town gossip circles. Josh Collmenter and Matt Powers, the heart and soul of the 2004 team, had graduated. Homer returned a boatload of talent, but replacing the leadership void of Collmenter and Powers would be more important than finding a pitcher who could deal with the big-game pressure. Although the Trojans had a lot on their plates as they reported for practice in the spring of 2005, it figured to be a much simpler season off the field. In some ways that would be true. There would be no more job controversy and no more lawyers or board meetings. But a crazy season was in store. Only this time it was a fun crazy.

Dusty Compton delivers.
*Photo by Doug Allen,
courtesy of the Battle Creek Enquirer.*

Into the National Limelight

Before the Trojans had a chance to defend their newly minted state title, the Salow brothers were forced to deal with more turmoil. This time it wasn't about jobs or arbitration cases or town politics. It was about their baseball mentor and friend, Spring Arbor coach Hank Burbridge. Grievances gave way to grieving as Burbridge's once-fit body was succumbing to cancer.

Hank and Pat Burbridge met in 1957 at Greenville College in southern Illinois. Hank, who hailed from little Pekin, Ill., and Pat, who called Chicago home, eventually married, moved to Michigan, and had a pair of daughters. In time, Hank grew into his job as Spring Arbor University baseball coach, and the family became entrenched in southern Michigan. Hank wanted to win as badly as the next guy, but he also had the ability to keep athletics in perspective. Years later, Burbridge's former players still remember that as vividly as any baseball lesson. "If the boys didn't leave here better than they came in morally, spiritually and socially, he felt he didn't do his job," Pat Burbridge said. "He was shaping young men for the future."

Tom Sharpley, who teamed with Chuck Finch to coach many of the Homer players when they were 11-15 years old, played at Spring Arbor under Burbridge in the late 1970s. Sharpley said Burbridge's greatest quality was that he was an honest, fair man. "He was more than just a baseball coach," Sharpley said. "He taught us about life issues."

In January 2005, Tom Salow walked downstairs to Scott's principal office and the two decided to call Burbridge's house and check up on his health. They were hoping his wife, Pat, would answer the phone so they could get an update with her before talking to their coach.

"I said, 'Hi, Mrs. Burbridge,'" Scott recalled. "But it ended up being coach so I felt bad. He still had his sense of humor right up until the end. I said this is a good chance for Tom and I to come over. We were going to leave right then in the middle of the school day. And he said, 'Well, I've got some visitors now and I'm gonna have some visitors later so I might be tired by then.'"

The high-school coach told his mentor "no problem," and maybe they could come over another time. About a week passed before Scott called again. This time Pat Burbridge answered and gave the grim news that her husband was not doing well. Pat passed the phone over to her sick husband for what would be the last conversation between a legendary small-college coach and the former player-turned-coach whom he considered the son he never had. "He said he was going to the hospital, and it's not good, Scotty," Scott Salow said. "He said, pray for me, buddy. And that was it. I didn't want to go over there anymore.

It was bad. It was just family."

Hank Burbridge spent his last living days at his home in Spring Arbor, in the town where he'd amassed 1,000 baseball wins and where the college field would later be renamed in his honor. It was mid-

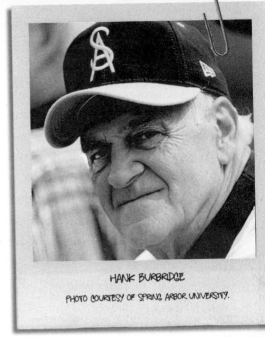

HANK BURBRIDGE
PHOTO COURTESY OF SPRING ARBOR UNIVERSITY.

February and Burbridge's oldest daughter, Patty, was home but his wife was not. Patty could tell her father was nearing his last moments when she said, "Dad, hang in there. Mom's not home. Wait for mom." Proving he had one last victory in him, the old coach kept fighting until his wife of 45 years arrived home to say goodbye. Pat Burbridge went to the bedroom and squeezed her husband's hand one last time before he passed away moments later.

Scores of Burbridge's former players, many of them with their own children now, flew back to Michigan to attend the coach's funeral. They laughed, cried, and told stories about the mentor that meant so much to so many. When Hank was sick, he received a get-well phone call from legendary Michigan football coach Bo Schembechler. It was one of many such kind gestures that came Burbridge's way in the final months of his rich life.

"Whenever he had a bad game, he never brought it home to us," Pat said. "The girls never saw an angry dad or coach. His daughters were very important to him. When Hank walked into a room, it just lit up. After he died, several coaches that I just knew by name talked about the magnetism he had about him. Little children and old people, they could all relate to him. People knew that he loved people."

"I was devastated," Sharpley said, getting emotional. "I looked at him as being invincible. I wish he were around today, I'd like to call and talk to him. I'd say, 'Hey coach' and he'd say, 'Tommy, how ya doing?'"

>>><<<

Homer began the 2005 season ranked No. 1 in Division 3, a spot it had grabbed and held onto for the second half of '04. Seven starters returned from a team that had made history with a 38-0 season. Still, Homer had some things to prove to itself. So far in high school, and even as Little Leaguers, this group of Homer players had been largely defined by Josh Collmenter and Matt Powers. In big postseason games, Collmenter and Powers would take the pressure off their younger teammates and welcome it squarely on their shoulders. Collmenter was always the big-game pitcher. Powers could always be counted on in the middle of the batting order. How would Homer deal without having its two leaders?

"They definitely set the mindset for our team," Dan Holcomb said of Collmenter and Powers. "When you're a freshman coming up you don't really know what varsity is all about or what Homer baseball is all about. You get up there and having those young guys playing against teams like Blissfield is kind of overwhelming. But having guys like Josh and Matt kept you loose and didn't let you think about Blissfield, or think about seven state titles [won by the Royals]. They just said, 'Hey guys, let's have some fun. We're going out to play some baseball today.' They just made sure everyone had their mind right."

Whether it was nerves about following up the unbeaten season with a good showing or an uneasy feeling taking the field without their two leaders, the Trojans began the new season with a close call in a doubleheader against Marshall and its star, Evan Sharpley. Marshall was a good team and a much bigger school, but Homer simply didn't have it. Somehow, the Trojans escaped with a 14-13 win in eight innings (the most runs it had given up in years) and then a 4-2 triumph in Game Two. With the first two wins under their belt, the Trojans began to roll. Over the next 12 games, they gave up a total of 13 runs, proof that the season opener was nothing more than a fluke. Collmenter and Powers were missing, but junior-dominated Homer began to form its own identity.

The state record for consecutive wins was 56, set by Grand Haven High School from 1960-62. Homer's Trojans were quickly nearing the record. The streak had reached 49 games when Homer took the short drive west on M-60 for a Big Eight tilt with the Union City Chargers. By now, the other teams in Homer's conference had basically ruled out beating the powerhouse. Goals such as scoring runs, playing all seven innings without the mercy rule, and even putting the ball in play against Homer's overpowering pitchers had become the scaled-down aspirations for the opponent.

One rival coach, Quincy's Brett Allman, didn't let his team watch Homer's impressive pregame routine where the Trojan players showed off their big-time throwing arms and precision fielding. "When they warmed up, I talked to my team outside the dugout, or had them hit Wiffle balls or something," Allman said. "Something besides watch them take infield. They put on a show. And they were proud of the way they took infield, and rightfully so. I don't need to watch Dusty Compton throw the ball across the infield because I know what they can do. I didn't think it would be real beneficial for my guys to watch them take infield."

Under gray, rainy skies in Union City, both teams finished their warm-ups and looked around. Something was missing. It was going to be hard to play this game without any umpires in sight. They waited and waited. Finally, around 5 p.m., 30 minutes after the scheduled start time, one ump arrived. Knowing how much less is seen on the field with only one umpire (regular-season high-school games have two), Salow was hesitant to let the game begin. The lone umpire told both coaches that his partner was on the way, so the coaches acquiesced and allowed the game to start with one set of eyes in charge of the entire field. Union City must've forgotten that its opponent that day had won 49 consecutive games. The Chargers came out like they were the team to beat and jumped all over Homer. A few innings into the game, Homer was stunningly down 7-0. "I said to Tom, 'Not only are we going to lose our streak but we're going to get 10-runned (a mercy rule loss),'" Salow said.

Of course, Homer started chipping away at the lead. But seven runs was a lot to come back from, even for these Trojans. In the fifth inning, with Homer still trailing by a few runs, C.J. Finch decided it was time to take control of the perilous situation. "Not today! Not today!" Finch screamed. "This is not going to happen today."

With rain continuing to fall, Homer got within one run in the sixth inning. That's when the umpire, who worked alone all game, walked over to Homer's dugout to speak with Salow.

"It's not looking good, starting to rain harder. Not sure if we're gonna be able to finish this thing," the ump told Salow.

"Absolutely not," the coach fired back. "We started this game 40 minutes late and if we'd started on time, it would be over by now. Not only that, but we have a streak going. These kids have worked too hard to put this streak together and they're not going to lose it this way."

The umpire caved in and so did Union City. Homer rallied to win 9-7, extending the winning streak to 50 games. Seven more remained to break the state record that had stood for 44 years.

"I was on pins and needles," Union City coach Joe Tinervia said of his team's near-miss. "I was playing that game like it was 1-0. That shows you what I think of Homer."

A few weeks later, Homer easily topped Concord 10-0 to tie Grand Haven's state record of 56 straight wins. The stage was set for the talented boys from the one-stoplight town to make history. A Friday doubleheader against Reading, one of the conference's better teams, would be the record-breaker. It seemed fitting, too, because Reading had handed Homer its last loss in a regional playoff game in 2003. Homer made history in a rather ho-hum affair, winning Game 1 of the doubleheader, 12-2. "It wasn't breathtaking or staggering or awe-inspiring," a *Battle Creek Enquirer* columnist wrote the next day. "But it was efficient. Forgive Homer if it didn't stage a large celebration for the new record. It's just that the boys are used to winning."

"It was just good enough, not flashy," Salow said after his team won its 57th straight baseball game. "I'd like to think we're a blue-collar club. It's the way guys are taught in practice and in the classroom. We try and never get too high or too low."

>>><<<

Homer was so affected by becoming a new state record holder that it only won Game 2 by a score of 17-1. In that game, Homer scored 10 runs in the first inning, including two home runs by Dale Cornstubble, who had three dingers on the day. Earlier in the day, during the Game 1 win, Dan Holcomb thought he had taken a walk but the home-plate umpire called a late strike. Holcomb had already tossed his bat toward the dugout, and it was a rare moment of unease for the rolling program. Afterward, Salow didn't let it slide. "That's not like Dan, and I was not happy about that," the coach said. "I'm sure as soon as he flipped that bat he knew he was in trouble.

That's not acceptable. It starts with me and it's a reflection of the program."

"In case you lost track, those sentiments were from the coach whose team has won 58 straight games," the *Enquirer* quipped.

"Consistency is the No. 1 thing that comes to mind," Reading coach Rick Bailey said about Homer. "They've been a program over the years, it's not something that happened overnight. It looks to me like every young kid in Homer wants to be a Trojan baseball player."

With the state record in tow, Homer continued on the task of winning another state championship:

Homer 15, Jonesville 0; streak reaches 59.
Homer 10, Columbia Central 0; streak reaches 60.
Homer 5, Quincy 2; streak reaches 61.
Homer 14, Quincy 6; streak reaches 62.
Homer 13, Onsted 0; streak reaches 63.
Homer 16, Jackson Parma Western 0; streak reaches 64.
Homer 18, Athens 0; streak reaches 65.
Homer 10, Union City 0; streak reaches 66.

Around this time, Salow got an unexpected phone call from an acquaintance, who delivered some very interesting news. Apparently, Salow was told, the current holder of the high-school national record for consecutive victories had just been knocked off. The team was La Cueva High School in Albuquerque, N.M., and shortly after staking claim to the national record in the spring, La Cueva's Bears had been beaten, halting their winning streak at 70 games. Holy Moses, Salow thought, we're five games away from owning that record!

>>><<<

Down in Albuquerque, Stan McKeever was understandably bewildered. As coach of the La Cueva Bears, McKeever had recently led the Bears on a glorious run though 5A baseball, New Mexico's biggest school classification. Unlike Michigan, high-school teams were only allowed to play 26 regular season games a year in New Mexico, and La Cueva had won three straight state titles. Only eight teams qualify for the state playoffs in the Land of Enchantment. The Bears' win streak lasted over parts of four seasons, while Homer's was less than two.

La Cueva had recently broken a national record that lasted for 39 years when it overtook New York's Archbishop Molloy High School's 68-game win streak from 1963-66. But the Bears won just once more after that, before regrouping to finish 28-1 and win a third consecutive state crown. La Cueva and Homer couldn't have been more different; earlier in the year, La Cueva had been named the 22nd-best athletic high school in the country by *Sports Illustrated*. Homer wasn't in the running for that list but it was awful close to stealing star-crossed La Cueva's potentially short-lived thunder.

Homer's streak reached 69 games, one short of the record, when it played in a Division 3 district playoff at Union City. The Trojans were 31-0, but their sights were on more than just a second-straight state title. National history was now within their reach. On a muggy June day, the village of Homer congregated on Union City's baseball field, about a 20-mile drive from Homer. They were no longer a baseball team. They were suddenly the biggest high-school sports story in America. With a likely doubleheader in store (Homer had to beat Albion in the district semifinal to advance to the district final later that day), fans of all ages wanted to see history being made. They wanted to say they were there.

"You might as well go because no one else is going to be here anyway," said Gale Smith, the barbershop owner.

"It inspired the town, it really did," said Gary Shrontz, owner since 1964 of Shrontz's Laundry Mat on Main Street. "Any small town would feel the same way. You just don't see that many good ballplayers at one time. It may never happen again. There's not too many people in town who weren't enthused by it."

So many people were on hand at Union City you had to arrive several hours early to secure a seat in the bleachers. Most fans were relegated to standing up alongside the fence next to the dugouts — not that they minded. Some fans showed real ingenuity by bringing lawn chairs and charcoal grills that they placed beyond the right-field wall, which provided a good vantage point.

In the morning district semifinal, the Trojans easily thumped overmatched Albion, 10-0. Homer now sat at 70 straight wins, a remarkable baseball achievement that tied it with La Cueva for the longest streak in high-school baseball history. Then they waited as host Union City got past Bronson, 5-2, setting up a

Homer vs. Union City district final. If people actually remembered this was a district final: more important, to everyone but the coaches, was the history.

Homer shortstop Ryan Thurston, a kind of unsung hero in all the team's glory, walloped a solo home run over the left-field fence in the first inning to put the Trojans on top. An inning later, Thurston came up again and this time delivered a three-run bomb to nearly the same place over left field. Homer led 6-0, and with stud junior Dusty Compton on the mound, the excitable crowd was just waiting for the inevitable history to be made. Union City actually scored three times off Compton in the third, cutting the lead in half, but it wouldn't get any closer than that. Homer scored twice more in the fourth, and when it put up a six-spot in the fifth inning, the Trojans were just three outs away from yet another mercy-rule triumph.

Union City's Dennis Shaffer strolled to the plate as the sun-splashed field hummed in anticipation. With two strikes on Shaffer, he offered at an outside pitch, and that was it. From humble beginnings to a national record, the Homer Trojans had won their 71st straight baseball game. No team in America had ever done it before. The players and coaches in orange mobbed each other on the mound as an appreciative crowd roared in approval after seeing what they hoped, and knew, would happen when they drove to the park this day.

"It's hard to grasp what we've done at the national level," Salow said to a large pool of newspaper and television reporters. "It's something that nobody can ever take from us. The longest streak in our country's history. That's a mouthful."

"We expected to win every game," said junior Brock Winchell. "Our chemistry was so good, it didn't matter who we played or what time of day it was. We kind of felt sorry for the other teams. We joked about it. I don't think a lot of teams felt they had a chance to win. That made it kind of easier for us because they laid down for us."

HOMER PLAYERS CELEBRATE THEIR NATIONAL RECORD-SETTING VICTORY AT UNION CITY. PHOTO BY MIKE WARNER, COURTESY OF THE HOMER INDEX.

The 71st straight win placed Homer on a different stratosphere than any high-school baseball team in recent memory. "I don't know what to say. We thought it might last for more than 40 days," La Cueva's McKeever said. "Some kids were a little disappointed. Personally, I tip my cap to [Homer]. I know how difficult it was for us to break it."

The record winning streak, plus the small-town charm, turned the Homer team into instant celebrities. Because they had set a national record, a few paragraphs on the achievement was sent across the country on the Associated Press wire, a service almost every daily newspaper and television station in America uses. Homer's baseball team was getting blurbs in random papers such as the *Louisville Courier-Journal* and the *Nashville Tennessean*. That was just the beginning.

In the week following the record win, Homer went from local to state to national story. The Trojans were mentioned in *Sports Illustrated*'s "Go Figure" section, *ESPN The Magazine*, *Baseball America*, and *USA Today*. They also got radio play on the *Paul Harvey Show*, and Salow was heard on the *Mitch Albom Show* on WJR radio in Detroit. More regionally, the *Detroit News* and *Detroit Free Press* came to town for stories on the small-town wonders.

The *Detroit News* story, which was accompanied by photos of Dan Holcomb, Dale Cornstubble, and Brandon Gibson, began with "Somewhere Abner Doubleday is smiling, knowing that a town called Homer is home to the nation's longest high-school winning streak."

>>><<<

All the attention had the 1,800 town residents in a tizzy. "I drove to Jackson to buy a *Detroit Free Press* because they were all sold out in Homer," said Ryan Cascarelli, the third-generation owner of Cascarelli's Pizza. "They are local celebrities. I feel sorry for them because every time somebody my age or older talked to them, it was only about baseball. They probably wanted to say, 'Put more pepperoni on my pizza,' but I wanted to talk baseball."

Gale Smith, the longtime barber, was one of many residents bursting with hometown pride as a group of teenage boys put

Homer on a national stage for the first time in its history. Also a car-racing fan, Smith was at the Chicago Speedway in Joliet, Ill., when he realized just how far-reaching his favorite baseball team had become. Smith was wearing his orange Homer baseball shirt at the race when a stranger approached him. "He says to me, 'Are you from Homer, Michigan, where they play baseball?'" Smith recalled. "I was proud to wear it. I was proud somebody knew it."

"Me, Cody Collmenter, and Brock Winchell were up at Central [Michigan] visiting Josh [Collmenter], and one of us had a Homer shirt on," C.J. Finch said. "A police officer comes up to us and says, 'Hey man, you guys are the team that had that good baseball team?' I said, 'Yeah, here's our starting pitcher and I'm the starting second baseman.' It was pretty neat. We get that a lot."

"Growing up your whole life, when you go somewhere else in the state you say, 'I'm from the Battle Creek area or I'm from Jackson.' You say one of the two cities," Dan Holcomb said. "After a while you say, 'I'm from Homer,' and people say, 'Oh, the baseball city.' It was a little different going from nobody had ever heard of it to everyone recognizes you. When you walk around town, everyone was talking about the baseball team."

The attention was about to increase tenfold. Homer was a few days away from its regional semifinal game against Bronson when Salow fielded a call from television giant ESPN. The ESPN rep told Salow that the network was working on a series called "50 States, 50 Days," and it was traveling the country looking for interesting stories with a local flavor. Someone tipped off ESPN about Homer's new record, and producers thought it would be a great segment for their Michigan show. "This is becoming insane," Salow thought to himself. "We still have a championship to win." Salow was told to be ready for ESPN cameras to be in his dugout when Homer played Manchester at the Bronson Regional in a few days. When the coach went to practice later that day, he had some mighty juicy news to deliver to the boys. He had to make sure they were ready to play baseball, too.

While Homer went through its always-crisp pregame routine for the regional semifinal against Manchester, there was a very abnormal process going on in its dugout. ESPN was setting up its cameras to shoot game footage of the Trojans for the series. Salow was worried about his team's concentration level. "How are these teenagers going to play their baseball if they're worried about looking good for *SportsCenter*?"

Salow might've been worried, but his team wasn't. With the ESPN cameras rolling from the dugout, Homer's players didn't miss a beat. The Trojans crushed Manchester 13-3 in the regional semifinal and a few hours later took care of Michigan Center, 10-0. It was Homer's 11th and 12th straight mercy-rule victories, sending the Trojans into the Division 3 quarterfinal round. The streak was now at 73 games. "It was a big relief to get to the ballpark," Salow told the *Citizen-Patriot*. "I told the boys, you're down to 32 teams, they're all good teams and we have to play well to advance. Now there are eight teams left and we're fortunate to be there."

Against Manchester in the regional semifinal, Cornstubble had six RBI in one inning, including a grand-slam homer, and finished 6-for-7 on the day. Holcomb picked up the win on the mound, improving to 16-0 on the year. In the final against Michigan Center, the Cascade Conference champion, Compton pitched a three-hitter to hand the team its first shutout defeat of the season. The Trojans did display a nice sense of timing with their speedy victory. Shortly after the game ended and parents snapped a few team pictures for the ever-growing scrapbook, a large storm hit Bronson that likely would have delayed play for some time. Luckily for Homer, it was already on the team bus heading home. As always, danger was in the rearview mirror, and Homer already had its sights set on hurdling the next obstacle.

Homer knew its streak of 10-run victories was likely to end. A familiar foe was waiting for them in two days. Just like last year, a berth to the State Semifinals at Battle Creek was going to be tough. And just like last year, the Blissfield Royals and their unmatched tradition would be the roadblock. Howell High School would provide the same venue for the quarterfinal match between two hungry teams, Homer and Blissfield. For players, coaches, and fans, the game couldn't get here quick enough.

Brock Winchell shows his frustration during the seemingly endless fourth inning.
Photo by Doug Allen, courtesy of the Battle Creek Enquirer.

Adversity & Grace

Though it had been a full year, the 2004 Homer-Blissfield classic was still fresh in everybody's minds. From Tuttle's pre-game comments about Collmenter to the Trojans' gritty perseverance in the seventh inning, the game had been epic. It had been a validation for the Trojans, who were sick and tired of hearing about their weak schedule and how they were scared of the big boys. Clinging to a 1-0 lead in the seventh, Blissfield loaded the bases before Collmenter got the final out, on a groundball to C.J. Finch. This time around, Homer didn't have the luxury of leaning on Collmenter. He was in college, though he'd be sure to be watching from the stands with the rest of his proud town.

Tuttle wasn't going to be giving Homer bulletin board material for the rematch, but he wasn't backing down either.

"We've scouted them a half-dozen times," Tuttle said. "I know everything there is to know. We're two ballclubs that are very much the same." Tuttle, ever looking for an edge, did think Blissfield had something that Homer couldn't match. "Our schedule, without reservation, other than maybe Lansing

Catholic Central, is the toughest in the state," Michigan's all-time winningest coach said. "Homer is an excellent ballclub, but we're not in awe of Homer. And Homer isn't in awe of us. Homer is another game on our schedule."

Salow didn't try to pretend this was just another game for his club. The Trojans had won 73 straight games, but the previous year's 1-0 triumph was likely their biggest and most satisfying, outside of the state title game. Of equal significance, it was also probably their most difficult. But with many of the same players back from last year, Salow used a familiar tactic to prepare his team. "My only message is that we don't have to beat Blissfield's tradition," Salow said. "We just have to score one more run than they do."

All the hype generated around Homer-Blissfield II was quickly becoming moot. The Homer Trojans, with a national streak intact and their eyes on a second-straight state title, opened the game looking like just another high-school baseball team. Or worse. After committing 26 errors in its first 35 games of the season, Homer was kicking the ball around like a mediocre J.V. outfit. The low point came when Compton tried to pick a runner off at first base with nobody covering the bag. The errant throw sailed into foul territory down the first-base line, allowing Blissfield's third run to score. In the third inning, Blissfield scored three runs on one hit and *four* errors. Homer's play was so uncharacteristically bad, few people in the jam-packed crowd realized what was brewing overhead. With Homer trailing 3-1 in the fourth inning, a vicious rainstorm hit Howell and halted play for nearly an hour.

The only thing worse than Homer's five errors in the first three innings was the team's attitude. Completely out of character, Homer was now bickering with each other as the realization sunk in that its season was awfully close to being over. "People were getting on each other, yelling at each other," senior Brandon Gibson told the *Citizen-Patriot.* "It's not good when you start yelling at people. You should encourage them. There's a time to get on someone, but not when you're down."

In the stands and behind the backstop, the scene was equally strange. Everyone wanted to know, "Is

GRACE IN ADVERSITY AS HOMER FANS EXPRESS THEIR APPRECIATION.
PHOTO COURTESY OF MHSAA.

this where it ends?" Homer's streak had brought even the most casual of sports fans out to the park. Now they were wondering if they'd be witness to history of another sort — the mighty streak falling. Up until the rain delay, Blissfield had been the confident team, while Homer couldn't do anything right. Blissfield's left-handed pitcher, Andrew Estes, had allowed just one run on two hits through Homer's first four innings at bat.

Compton wasn't pitching horribly, but he couldn't overcome the lackluster fielding behind him. After nearly an hour delay, with the entire crowd still waiting, the umpires resumed play with Blissfield leading 3-1.

With the Royals batting first — as the home team they hit in the bottom of the fourth — Compton re-entered the game like a different player. Homer's emotional right-hander had as crisp a fastball as he'd had all year. His curveball was a gorgeous tightly spinning parabola rendering Blissfield hopeless. Compton struck out the side in the fourth, and Homer began to feel like Homer again.

"I think it kind of got us back down to Earth," Cornstubble said of the rain delay. "You get this feeling that you know you're going to win when you win 74 games in a row. You just know something good is going to happen."

There was still plenty of work to do before win No. 74 could be officially recorded. Blissfield's Estes, still pitching after the rain delay, continued to mow down Homer's hitters. Compton was doing his part, too, but this was going to require some hitting to get back in the game. In Homer's half of the sixth inning, things finally started to fall into sync for the Trojans. Dan Holcomb hit a sacrifice fly to right field, scoring Ryan Thurston and narrowing Blissfield's lead to 3-2. That's when the Homer karma took over.

Next up was Brandon Gibson, who took first base after being struck by Estes with an 0-2 pitch. The game-tying run was now at third base (Cornstubble) as No. 7 hitter Cody Collmenter strolled to the plate. By all accounts, Cody Collmenter was a heckuva nice kid and decent athlete, but he'll never be confused with his brother Josh. While Josh was a superstar and record-setting pitcher, Cody was a role player, a bottom-of-the-order guy who played left

THE HOMER CROWD CELEBRATES ANOTHER STRIKEOUT DURING THE LANSING DIAMOND CLASSIC
PHOTO COURTESY OF LANSING STATE JOURNAL.

field. None of that mattered as Cody settled into the box for the biggest at-bat of his young life. Try as he might, Cody was over-matched by Estes. With two strikes, Cody swung and missed at a low pitch, and Blissfield appeared to be out of the inning, still clinging to a one-run lead. But the inning wasn't over quite yet. As Cody whiffed at the pitch, the ball hit the front lip of home plate and flew over Royals catcher Will Faulkner all the way to the backstop. With both sides of the crowd going nuts, Cornstubble raced home to tie the game 3-3, and Cody Collmenter took first base with a dropped-third-strike he'll never forget.

Next up was number-eight batter Brock Winchell, who slammed a line-drive single to left field, scoring two runs to give Homer a 5-3 advantage. "That rain delay didn't help us any," Tuttle said. "Homer has been down before. And then they had a chance to regroup. The game was over for all practical purposes when they scored the four runs in the sixth."

Blissfield had two more innings to mount a comeback, but Tuttle's statement was basically correct. The way Compton was pitching, lots of college teams would've had trouble scoring. After the rain delay, Compton and his electric stuff retired 12-consecutive batters, and Homer lived to play another day. Players and coaches mobbed one another after Compton retired the final hitter, showing a sense of relief and amazement at their latest accomplishment. Even for a group that was accustomed to major victories, this was special. Two straight years, the Trojans sent Blissfield back east for a somber bus ride. Compton, now 15-0, finished with 11 strikeouts and just two hits allowed.

Homer 5, Blissfield 3.

The Trojans' streak was now at 74 straight games. They were 36-0 on the year and two wins away from a second straight Division 3 state title. But things got dicey on this rainy day in Howell. "In the first couple innings we were showing signs that we might be nervous," Salow said. "We made four errors in one inning. We never do that. I think the rain delay really gave us a chance to regroup."

In addition to its regular game story, the *Battle Creek Enquirer* did an atmosphere piece with quotes from fans. There were tons to choose from, all in orange shirts, of course, and they were a happy group after another win over mighty Blissfield. "There might be one police officer left in town," said fan Debbie Chard. "And my son is up there in the stands and he knows one person that didn't come. But my son keeps calling him with updates."

With Blissfield behind them for the second straight year, the Trojans were back in the Division 3 semifinals at Battle Creek's Bailey Park. Here a whole new challenge awaited them: the little team that could. The Watervliet Panthers, a school on the west side of the state near Lake Michigan, might have been the least probable team to reach the Final Four in any of the four divisions. Watervliet coach Aaron Hyska had gone 11-23 in his first year at the school, but now in season four his Panthers were two wins from a state title. Furthermore, Watervliet had entered the state playoffs with a 16-13 record, only to get hot at the right time and reel off six straight postseason wins. The real surprise came in the quarterfinal round when Watervliet shocked the state by knocking off perennial power Lansing Catholic Central, 5-1.

The hype or lack thereof was quite a change for Homer. Against Blissfield, fans and players alike knew the opponent, its coach, and the top players' names. There was a history from the previous year and a general rivalry built in, Old Power versus New Record Setter. Watervliet, even with its intriguing playoff run, couldn't provide any of that same drama Tuttle's Royals had brought to the table. Still, it didn't take long to realize that the surprise team from near the shores of Lake Michigan wasn't just going to hand over Homer's 75th straight win.

Batting first as the road team, Watervliet scored one run in the first inning off of Holcomb. Homer countered with three in its half of the first and then two more in the second. It was shaping up like another Homer rout until Watervliet came to bat in the top of the third inning. Holcomb, the marvelous righty who entered the game 16-0, wasn't his usual sharp self. The Panthers pounded four hits off Holcomb in the third inning and scored four runs to tie the score, 5-5. Homer was on the ropes, but another unlikely hero was about to emerge. Against Blissfield, it had been eighth-place hitter Brock Winchell rising to the occasion. This time, it would be Kyle Meeks, batting in the ninth spot. The scrappy center fielder and all-around athlete was also known as an excellent defensive back on the football team. With two outs in the bottom of the third and Homer leading 6-5, Meeks singled in two huge runs to give the Trojans an 8-5 cushion. Later that inning, he would come around to score, and Homer was well on its way.

From there, Holcomb settled down and didn't allow another run. He finished with nine strikeouts and two walks. Although it was far from his finest outing, Holcomb was

KYLE MEEKS MAKES A BIG PLAY IN THE OUTFIELD.
PHOTO BY ROD SANFORD, COURTESY OF THE LANSING STATE JOURNAL

good enough and his offense made sure of it. Holcomb finished with two RBI at the plate, as did Thurston and Meeks, and the Trojans cruised to an 11-5 victory. Watervliet committed five errors, a sin that could simply not be overcome against a Homer team that had returned to its fundamentally sound form. It might've looked like another close call from the stands, especially to a fan base that watched its team pitch a state-record 21 shutouts. But that's not how the players saw it. "There was no doubt today," C.J. Finch said after his team won its 75th straight game. "It was just another game."

Salow wasn't as satisfied. Homer wasn't playing its best baseball at the end of the year, and that had its coach concerned. Sure, they appeared headed for another undefeated season, but Salow felt Homer should clobber a team like Watervliet. Coasting to an 11-5 victory would be fine with most coaches, but Salow was accustomed to seeing near-perfection. "I'm half-tempted to go back to practice," Salow said after the game. "We're a good defensive team, but we haven't showed that the last couple of games. We showed signs of cracking a little bit and that worries me."

Homer had committed only two errors against Watervliet, not a huge number for high-school baseball, but more than a championship-level team should be happy with. "I don't know what it is," C.J. Finch said. "I don't know if it's nerves or what but we don't make those errors. I expect [at the title game] we'll be focused and ready to play." The sloppy play didn't affect Finch's confidence for win No. 76 and clinching state title No. 2. "We didn't come into the season looking for a national record. We came into this looking to win a state champion-ship," Finch said.

The kids who had become celebrities in their town, who had given its community a reason to puff out its collective chest, were now on the brink of a second-consecutive state championship. Maybe because they were so talented and well schooled, Homer looked like it was playing the same carefree baseball it always had. But in truth, these kids were dragging. For the second straight year, they were playing on the final possible day of the high-school season — 76 games in all over two years. Maybe more significantly, the entire team had played through more pressure than most high-school baseball teams could imagine. It's not that the team was playing not to lose, but it wasn't really high-school athletics anymore. Every game played was a big deal, something of a town meeting. Every record was another headline, another performance to live up to the next time out at the ball yard. Inning-by-inning perfection was almost required as the wins piled up.

No doubt, Homer was still having fun playing baseball. But for the last month it just felt different. The small-town friends who thrived in their familiar bubble suddenly felt like their every move was under a microscope.

>>><<<

"I don't think anyone can imagine what the guys had to go through in 2004, and especially the 2005 season," Salow said. "It was every day, newspapers and cameras and interviews. Today this newspaper's here, so Cody and Brock speak. And tomorrow, this newspaper's here, so Danny and Ryan speak. It was almost assigning guys speaking engagements. To have to play under that kind of pressure … as coaches we tried to not talk about the streak. We tried to keep things simple.

"To stay on an even keel in the situations these guys have been placed in front of … then you remember that they're 16- and 17-year-olds," Salow continued, "I can't say enough about their mental makeup."

On the other side of the Division 3 bracket, Saginaw Nouvel defeated Leroy Pine River, 5-1, in the semifinal. Nouvel improved to 29-13 with the win, which was something of a one-man show by Blair White. White tossed a complete-game two-hitter against Pine River, striking out six without walking a batter. White retired the last nine batters he faced and also went 2-for-3 with three RBI at the plate. Privately, Salow was somewhat shocked that Nouvel used White, its ace, in the semifinal. Homer's coach figured Nouvel could win the semifinal without its star pitcher, which would allow White to pitch in the state title game. Salow didn't know who Saginaw Nouvel would throw against his Trojans now.

John Johnson, the MHSAA's director of communications, still has a picture hanging in his Lansing office taken during the first inning of the Homer-Saginaw Nouvel championship game. The scene was mesmerizing for a high-school baseball game, especially one between two smallish schools. Homer's orange-shirted fans took over Battle Creek's C.O. Brown Stadium. Johnson estimates that a state-record crowd of more than 4,000 people was in attendance.

"That picture has a big sea of orange and a tiny speck of blue [Nouvel's colors]," Johnson said. "When you talk about communities, you capture the essence of what we're all about. The fact that Homer developed a great following over this time doesn't surprise me. When you get a winning streak, you get the focus [of attention], not only a state record but also a national record. This was one of those, 'Empty out the town, last one turn off the lights,' kind of moments. It's what makes it fun. When you hear about streaks like this, a lot of times they become a passing thing. For whatever reason, Homer stood out in your mind. It had the kind of drawing power I've only seen a few times."

Since Holcomb pitched Friday's semifinal, fellow ace right-hander Dusty Compton would be taking the ball for Homer against Nouvel. At 15-0, Compton had a bit more big-game experience than Holcomb, but the two were essentially interchangeable. The fiery Compton had retired both batters he faced against Shepherd in the 2004 state title game when Collmenter only had 6 ⅓ innings available to pitch. A year later, Salow handed the ball to Dusty from the start and asked him to be himself. Dusty, who wore excessive eye black that just about resembled Gene Simmons from the rock band Kiss, was one of the state's most dominant pitchers when he was sharp. Salow and the thousands of Homer fans were counting on another typical Dusty outing.

Salow felt as confident as ever as he trotted toward home plate to meet with the umpires and Saginaw Nouvel coach Tim Smith for the standard pregame meeting on ground rules.

Salow handed over his lineup card, the one that had hardly changed in two years:

1. Finch, second base
2. Thurston, shortstop
3. Cornstubble, catcher
4. Compton, pitcher
5. Holcomb, first base
6. Gibson, right field
7. C. Collmenter, left field
8. Winchell, third base
9. Meeks, center field

Homer was the road team, and the feverish crowd gave its first loud wail of the day when Holcomb connected on an RBI single to give the Trojans a 1-0 lead in the first inning. In the fourth, Compton, ever one for big-stage theatrics, drilled a home run about 340 feet over the wall in left-center field to lead off the inning. By inning's end, Homer had scored three more times and held a commanding 5-0 advantage over Nouvel and its starting pitcher Nick Szott. If ever a crowd felt its team's game was in the bag, this was it.

"Winning 5-0 in the fourth, we're 12 outs away," Salow said later. "We're feeling good because we just don't give up runs."

But in the bottom half of the fourth inning, Compton ran into trouble. While Nouvel wasn't an imposing bunch, it was a scrappy team that put the ball in play. Nouvel's Blair White led off the inning with a triple down the line. After a strikeout, Nouvel ripped four straight hits to make the score 5-2 with the bases loaded. C.J. Finch committed an error on a potential double-play ball, followed by another single and a bases-loaded walk to tie the game. That's when Salow replaced Compton on the mound with Dan Holcomb, who had pitched seven innings the day before in the semifinal versus Watervliet. Holcomb struck out the first batter, but then allowed Matt Kretz, in his second at-bat of the inning, to hit a two-run bloop single just out of Finch's reach to give Nouvel a 7-5 lead. The ball appeared destined for Finch's glove until the second baseman made one false move in, allowing the ball to graze just past his mitt on a leaping attempt. Kretz's hit, which came on a 3-2 count, was his team's fourth two-strike hit of the inning. In all, Nouvel had knocked around Homer's best for seven hits and seven runs in the inning.

A comfortable 5-0 lead had oh-so-quickly turned into a two-run deficit as Homer retreated to its dugout for the top of the fifth. The Trojans hadn't been challenged quite like this in a non-Blissfield game during the past two years. While Homer was the prohibitive favorite entering the state championship game, apparently someone forgot to let Nouvel in on the secret. The Panthers were playing like they were the ones featured in *USA Today* and on the *Paul Harvey Show*.

How would Homer respond? With its three, four, and five hitters up in the fifth inning, it seemed like this was the time to strike back for the Trojans. That theory failed to come through, though, as Nouvel's Szott continued to keep Homer's hitters off balance. Leading off the inning, Cornstubble grounded out to third. That was followed by Compton's flyout to right and Holcomb's strikeout looking. All of a sudden, Nouvel was six outs away from toppling Michigan's small-school Goliath.

Holcomb, using the few bullets that remained in his fatigued right arm, retired Nouvel 1-2-3 in the bottom of the fifth. But Nouvel wanted no part of this Cinderella story. Once again in the sixth, Szott sent Homer's hitters back in order to the now-distraught dugout. Holcomb got out of a minor jam in the sixth, and the stage was set. Homer's nine players raced in from its positions in seven seconds or less and readied for whatever awaited them. Down two runs, the Trojans needed Blissfield-like heroics to pull this thing out. Everyone in orange believed they'd do it. Down in the third-base coaching box, Salow had his own set of unique thoughts.

"I remember taking my hat off, I've got No. 20 [his jersey number] written in there, and I remember looking at the number," he said. "I wanted to make sure that if it was meant to be, that our kids acted appropriately. That's all I wanted. Do this the right way, win or lose."

It wasn't over yet. True to form, Homer rallied. Kyle Meeks grounded out to start the inning, but the gritty Finch drilled a single to right field to get it going. Next up, Thurston hammered a double to right-center, and the Trojans had runners on second and third with one out. Nouvel's skipper Tim Smith called upon his ace, taking out Szott and bringing in Blair White from first base to pitch. As if it were scripted, Homer had its best hitter, the incomparable Dale Cornstubble, at the plate. Cornstubble couldn't find a hole, though, and instead flew out to right field, scoring Finch, but placing Homer one out from the unthinkable — a loss. Trailing 7-6 with Thurston at third base, Dusty Compton walked up to the plate with revenge on his mind. Compton would never forgive himself for getting shellacked in the fourth inning of the state championship game, but a hit here would certainly ease the pain. With the town of Homer on its feet, one of its favorite sons took his place in the right-handed hitters' box. Compton got an outside pitch and hammered it — right at Nouvel second baseman Craig Riffel. Riffel calmly fielded the ball, tossed over to first base, and the Nouvel celebration was on. Saginaw Nouvel 7, Homer 6.

For the first time in 76 games, the Homer Trojans lost. Complete shock was almost palpable, both on the field and in the stands. Gone was the national win streak. Gone, too, was a second straight state title that almost felt inevitable. Nobody knew what to feel, think or say.

"When it happened, the first thing I wanted to do was observe how my kids were acting," Salow said. "The only one was Dusty, because he made the last out and was the pitcher of record. He had his helmet in his hand and was about to chuck it at someone, somebody, something, and he was the only one who showed any sign of weakness. I said, 'Dusty, we're not going out like that.' And he came up to me later that day and apologized. That was really important to me. We're not going to throw equipment. Our fans gave us a standing ovation."

Even the final out itself was unusual to a team that didn't know what losing felt like. "It was weird because Dusty pulls everything," Salow said. "He *never* hits one to second. Maybe five times in his career. But he hit it hard. The second baseman barely got his glove down." Homer's legion of supporters filed out of C.O. Brown Stadium with a blank stare on their faces. "Nobody saw it coming," said Ryan Cascarelli. "That was talked about as much as the winning. The team handled the loss better than the community did. We were sad."

Homer's players cried, hugged, and stared stunningly at the scoreboard that looked foreign to them. Right fielder Brandon Gibson was the only senior in Homer's starting lineup, so the team would be ferocious next year, but this wasn't a time to think about the future. The Trojans just couldn't believe that some way, somehow, they didn't squeeze out their 76th straight victory.

"I'm just thinking about all the things we could have done," Finch said. "It's a heartbreaker for the fans, players and coaches. We thought we were going to pull it out in the end. This should have been a game we won, but we didn't."

Across the field, Nouvel coach Tim Smith was explaining how his team had knocked off the Trojans. Luck, Smith said, had nothing to do with it. "We talked about the game itself," Smith said of his pre-game speech. "Records don't win you a game. I don't think the streak will ever be broken. And they'll be back, too."

While his players packed up and slowly walked off the field to join family and friends, Salow probably set a record for most reporters interviewing a losing coach at a Michigan high-school baseball game. "It will sting for a few hours, probably a few days," he said. "But we got back to a place a lot of people said we couldn't get back to. We won 75 consecutive games and fell one run short. Life's been pretty good for us still."

A few years after the fact, the Nouvel loss resonates with Homer's players as much as any win. Just mention the game and the player invariably will look downward or shake his head. Despite all the winning, it's the rare loss that still leaves a sour taste in the players' mouths. "The game of baseball is a funny game, and it was definitely going against us that day," Cornstubble said. "We thought we had the game in the bag, and all of a sudden, that one inning killed us. It took the wind out of our sails. If I would've come through and gotten a base hit, it would've tied it up …"

Not surprisingly, Homer's de facto team spokesman, Dan Holcomb, put the loss into proper context. "It felt bad because it was just one inning. We knew we should've played better. But by the same token, everyone just knew it was one game and we were bound to lose it. The bad part was that it was for the state title. That one state title was what hurt. We wanted to do it without Josh [Collmenter] and Matt [Powers]. As much as we liked those guys, we wanted to do it on our own. It just kind of let you down. You're right there and just couldn't do it."

It was the fourth state title for Saginaw Nouvel, which also beat Homer in the 1990 Class C championship game.

When the hugs from moms and strategic discussions with dads concluded, Homer's players solemnly boarded the team bus back to town. This wouldn't be nearly as enjoyable as the team's last three Battle Creek to Homer trips (this year's semi-final and two games in 2004). Emotional tears filled the bus as teenagers and coaches alike tried to make sense out of what just happened. Salow, for his part, was proud of the way his team dealt with defeat. That was as important to the coach as anything. When his brother Tom took the program over back in 1992, it was about playing the game right and respecting the game. Having learned from the Burbridge system as well, Scott felt the same way. You might not like the outcome of a particular game, but that doesn't give you the right to disrespect baseball. Never has and never will, according to the Salow boys. On this day when his team's winning streak ended at 75 and Scott Salow lost his bid for a second straight state championship, he learned that all those life lessons being taught at practices and team-bonding trips over the years had been, in fact, heard. It's always hard to know if teenagers are listening, but Salow's speeches hadn't fallen on deaf ears. In a strange sense, it was a proud moment for Salow.

As the bus exited I-69 and pulled onto M-60 heading east into town, the players felt the pit of their stomachs like never before after an athletic contest. Salow walked back down the bus aisle and attempted to console his players, telling them they were still champions, even if it didn't feel like it today. He told them to head over to assistant coach Rob Ridgeway's house, where there would be food and pop for what was expected to be another championship celebration. The kids could jump in the Ridgeways' pool, play with the coaches' kids, and get their mind off the day's events. As the bus neared Homer, one player nudged another. Like dominoes, another player tapped someone else's shoulder. "Look outside," one said. "What's going on out there?"

>>><<<

Homer High School might not have beaten Saginaw Nouvel for the 2005 state title, but Homer's residents felt as much pride as ever. Despite the loss, the town was giving the team an old-fashioned "Welcome Home" parade, replete with fire trucks and community members lining the streets. "It was one of those things where you didn't want to see anybody, you didn't want to talk to anybody," Holcomb said. "But at the same time you understood what it meant to the community. You didn't really want to smile, you wanted to go off into your car and go home. But the support felt good at the same time."

And support they did, as fans yelled and kids screamed to welcome back their national record-setting team. If the sign of a true fan is one who supports even in defeat, then the village of Homer showed its true colors in a faithful way on this Saturday afternoon.

"I said, 'You know, guys, we had quite a crowd today and people followed us from all walks of life; and now they're lining the streets,'" Salow recalled. "It's one of those days that you have as a champion or when you're dead — and I know we're neither today — but make these people happy and wave out the window."

Brent Holcomb, the superintendent and father of Dan, stood among the locals cheering on their defeated heroes. A former athlete himself, Holcomb rarely missed one of Dan's games, home or away. He was not a father who yelled instruction from the bleachers or scolded the coach for a failed scoring opportunity. Instead, Holcomb watched quietly while his son excelled under the leadership of the man he backed several months ago, Scott Salow. Even though Dan's athletic achievements were numerous, the town's support after the Nouvel loss remains one of Brent's favorite baseball-related memories. "I was so struck by how much the community embraced those kids," Brent said. "I thought that was pretty special. I relished being a part of that and all the things that went on with the team."

The way in which Salow handled defeat gracefully furthered Holcomb's belief that he made the right decision in publicly defending Salow's holding of principal and baseball coaching duties. Back then it was a delicate time for the superintendent as vocal critics decried his decision as only caring about baseball, or worse, not caring enough at all. Now, as Holcomb watched from afar while Salow's leadership and character qualities rubbed off on his players — when acting up would have been easy — it was a sort of confirmation of Holcomb's stance all along

"The thing I'm most appreciative of for Dan is what Scott gave him as a human being with integrity and hard work," Brent said. "[Salow] was never a yeller or a screamer. He always talked about what was best as a team. Playing for Scott, I think

Dan really grew as a young man. My son benefited so much as a person. Each kid is a sculpture waiting to happen, and each kid was shaped by that team. What parent, what person, would not want their kids to play for Tom and Scott Salow? They play sports the right way. Everything was in the right perspective. They take as much pride in being Academic All-State as they do in a state championship."

Homer's players mustered up some energy and trudged over to the Ridgeways' house for postgame food and reminiscing. Only a few hours earlier, they'd had one bad inning and it was enough to lose a national winning streak and a state championship. Of course, getting past this loss was going to be hard, especially with all the plays and miscues so fresh in their memory. Yet, despite all that, as the sun set on this June afternoon back in their small-town comfort zone among friends and family, the Homer players proved they hadn't lost all their innocence. Before long, they were throwing each other in the pool, laughing and joking again like the anonymous teenagers they once were. They were kids being kids; no cameras, no interviews, no pressure. "And life was going to be OK," Salow said.

The next morning Salow reluctantly picked up the day's newspapers to read what went wrong during the previous afternoon in Battle Creek. If losing a state title game wasn't bad enough, Salow was thoroughly shocked by a headline that ran on the front of the *Jackson Citizen-Patriot*'s sports section. Just beneath the standard game story, the *Citizen-Patriot*'s Gary Kalahar, who had covered many of Homer's feats during the past few seasons and who had a good relationship with Salow, wrote a column titled, "Trojans should not move into a lower division in 2006."

Weeks earlier, Homer had learned that because of a drop in enrollment for the following school year, it would dip from Division 3 to Division 4 in baseball. Moves like this happened all the time in Michigan, in all sports. If a school has a particularly small or big incoming freshman class, it can alter the school's enrollment one way or the other, thus relegating a division move as warranted by the MHSAA. Only in the very rare instance when a school asks for permission from the MHSAA would it remain in the old, larger-school division.

In Michigan, schools are placed in divisions on a sport-by-sport basis. Some sports are called divisions while others are classes. For instance, when Homer moved to Division 4 baseball, it remained in Division 7 football and Class C basketball. So the move down in baseball did not affect other sports.

Yet, as Salow was healing his wounds from the previous day's 7-6 defeat, he read this lead to Kalahar's column: "Imagine the Detroit Pistons, after two straight appearances in the NBA Finals, playing in the CBA next year. Or the Boston Red Sox returning to the World Series this fall and then going after the Triple-A crown the next season. Silly? Of course. Just about as silly as Homer High School playing in back-to-back state championship games in Division 3 baseball, and then, playing in the Division 4 tournament next year."

"I thought the article and its timing were unfair," Salow said later. "We had just watched our second undefeated state championship run and 75-game win streak end abruptly, and the next day the lead article is about the 2006 team playing down a division. The article made it sound like we chose to go down and not that it was enrollment based. Later on I had learned that during the state title game, interviews were being done of the Homer community and fans. For all the kids on that team had accomplished, this seemed like an inappropriate time to conduct controversial interviews."

The column discussed how Homer endured criticism for its perceived weak schedule but how that could be chalked up to pure jealousy. "Homer did not create a schedule with thoughts of racking up a winning streak," Kalahar wrote. "The Trojans play for championships, and you can't argue with the results. But if Homer elects to remain in Division 4, it will open itself up to criticism that is absolutely justified. Over the past two seasons, Homer has proven it is one of the best baseball programs in the state. But if its next trip to Battle Creek comes in Division 4, it will be cheapened."

As a 10-year veteran at the *Citizen-Patriot*, Kalahar wasn't surprised to catch some grief from Homer supporters for the column. Salow didn't confront him on the issue but others did. Still, Kalahar, who says covering Homer's amazing baseball run was one of the top stories he's ever seen on the prep beat, stands by his reasoning for the post-state tournament column. "My feeling was that those kids being placed in Division 4 was a no-win situation for them," Kalahar said later. "They had already dominated in Division 3 for two years. There was so much garbage out there on *Mlive.com* (the Booth newspapers Web site in Michigan, which has message board forums, including a baseball page where Homer was routinely criticized) and all that stuff. I don't pay that much attention, I think it's a bunch of garbage, but it's out there. There was all that criticism out there about the schedule to begin with. People saying the streak was bogus because they don't play anybody. If they win in Division 4, critics are going to say, 'So what?' And if they lose, oh man, they'd never hear the end of that. They'd say, 'Look at Homer, they're supposed to be so good and they can't even win Division 4.'"

Kalahar later said he understood some people taking issue with the timing of his column, but with the baseball season ending, this was the last chance to make the newsworthy point relevant. "This was a totally unique situation that Homer was in," Kalahar said. "No one in the nation had ever won 75 games in a row. I'm not sure Blissfield had ever gone to the state championship game three years in a row. I wasn't asking them to play up, I was asking them to stay where they are. They should stay where they dominated."

As he had done during the Salow-Finch arbitration case, *Homer Index* editor/publisher Mike Warner publicly weighed in on Kalahar's column. Warner wrote a response to Kalahar's column and sent it to the *Citizen-Patriot*, hoping that they'd run it on the editorial page. But according to Warner, the Jackson paper wouldn't print the letter, citing factual errors that were not specified. Unlike the average letter writer, Warner had other options. "Because I believe the column deserves a response, I'm printing my letter here — it's one of the perks of owning your own newspaper," Warner wrote in the *Index*. "It obviously won't have the same impact as running in the *Cit-Pat*, but it's the best I can do."

Warner's letter argued that Homer was being singled out for not staying in Division 3, when other schools had done the same thing. His main argument centered on Jackson Lumen Christi High School, a private-school football powerhouse that had won several state titles in recent years. Being a private school, Lumen Christi is allowed to pull players from other school districts to play for its football team. They've long been accused of recruiting, though Catholic schools across the country have been utilizing that practice for decades. Lumen Christi has around 700 students in its high school but regularly fields what amounts to an All-Star football team that pounds schools with much larger enrollments. Yet, come time for the state playoffs, the Lumen Christi Titans can be found competing in Divisions 5 or 6, based on their smallish enrollment. Why, Warner questioned, aren't there articles questioning the validity of that? Why pick on the little school that's had a two-year run of baseball glory?

"Homer isn't the only team in the state returning talented baseball players this year, but not a single baseball team in the state is playing up a classification this year, according to the MHSAA," Warner wrote. "Why single out Homer?"

Warner also wrote that if and when Homer brought home a Division 4 state title the following spring, they would be able to do it with their heads held high. "They will be a Division 4 team winning a Division 4 title. That might not be enough of an accomplishment for the *Cit-Pat*, but it is plenty for the Homer community."

>>><<<

Normally, Homer would've turned in its uniforms on Monday, signaling the official end of an unbelievable 37-1 season. For better or worse, "normal" and "Homer baseball" never did go well together. Salow would not be collecting uniforms on Monday. That's because he needed his players to be wearing them at their home field on Tuesday afternoon. Despite the loss to Nouvel, Homer was still going to be featured on ESPN's "50 States in 50 Days" series, and the media giant was coming to Homer High on Tuesday to shoot footage. When ESPN says they want the kids in their uniforms, then that's what they get.

Three days after the most disheartening loss of their young careers, the Trojans pretended it never happened. They ran through some practice drills, certainly the first-ever "mock practice" after a season in state history. ESPN interviewed several players, including C.J. Finch, Dan Holcomb, Brandon Gibson, and Brock Winchell. They interviewed Salow as well and staged some classic television spots where the team walks toward the camera in a straight line, looking ever-so-determined in their orange jerseys. Michigan's turn in the "50 States in 50 Days" finally came on Sunday, July 31. Thanks to a late major-league baseball game, though, the village of Homer was up well past its bedtime on that Sunday. A game between the Chicago White Sox and Baltimore Orioles lasted more than three hours, so *SportsCenter* didn't begin until after midnight, Eastern Standard Time. The boys might've been antsy but they sure weren't going to bed. At last, in the middle of the show, "50 States in 50 Days," flashed across the screen to millions of viewers worldwide as ESPN's Scott Van Pelt introduced Homer's story from a set on the edges of the Warwick Hills Golf and Country Club, host of the Buick Open.

"Just over 100 miles west of Detroit, there's a place called Homer, Michigan, a village of 1,800 people," Van Pelt began, using his hands to emphasize his points. "In 2004, their boys' baseball team won the Division 3 state title. In 2005, they received a great deal of national attention for their continued excellence on the diamond. Matt Winer explains why this team has been, if you will, a grand slam for Homer."

The segment began with Homer's entire team, including coaches and numerous bat boys (there were so many little kids in Homer's dugout, the players began referring to them as "Homer's day care") walking toward the camera in a dramatic shot. The boys have serious looks on their faces as they walk the home infield they've footed so many times before. Then ESPN's Winer says, "For the last two years, just like the sun being counted on to rise, the Homer, Michigan, baseball team could be counted on to win." With highlights of Homer hitters and pitchers playing, Winer describes the group's accomplishments of a national win streak and a state title. The cameras were still rolling at the state title game and there's a shot of Compton blasting his solo home run. The game footage ends with Homer standing around, stunned as Nouvel rushes the field after the championship game. Some of Homer's players are crying, too.

The piece, which runs a little over three minutes, ends with a few lines from Salow. "To be placed under a microscope like that team has been placed, 75 straight times, 'You've got to win, you've got to do it, you've got to win,' and they did it for us," Salow said. "They did it for themselves and the community and for little Homer High School. It's meant a lot to us and it's probably forever changed our lives."

Michigan's portion of "50 States in 50 Days," for which Homer was just one part, also included the PGA's Buick Open in Grand Blanc, near Flint, and other sports items from the Great Lakes State. "It was amazing," said C.J. Finch. "To think I watch *SportsCenter* every day and to think we're actually on it. Having all that media, it's just a great experience. Not many kids get to go through that. I'd like to think it helped the town a little bit. Honestly, I think it did help. There are a lot of people out there nowadays that know Homer because of what we did on the baseball field."

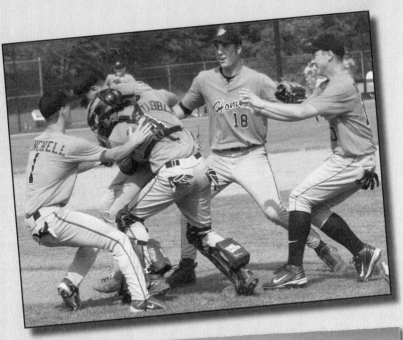

The Trojans celebrate after setting the national record with a win over Union City.

Photo by John Grap, courtesy of the Battle Creek Enquirer

A Time to Grow

Nobody took the loss to Saginaw Nouvel harder than C.J. Finch. Not only had Finch been involved with two of the game's biggest plays that went against Homer, but he was also one of the team's most competitive players among a group filled with tough, fiery kids. A smart kid and very good student, Finch knew there were dozens of plays in a baseball game and the outcome usually isn't decided by one or two. Still, the gutsy kid with the intense father couldn't get the botched double play and soft liner that barely got over his glove out of his mind.

Finch grew up around athletics, always tagging alongside his dad to football fields and baseball diamonds. Chuck Finch coached football and baseball for years, and young C.J. was never far behind. Chuck Finch played on the Homer men's softball team that went to Garland, Texas, and won a national championship in 1994. Not surprisingly, little C.J. was the team's batboy. Admittedly, Chuck was a tough, in-your-face man and some of his intensity rubbed off on C.J. The younger Finch wasn't as loud as his father, but make no mistake, the super-quick, 5-foot-7 athlete wanted to win as badly as anybody.

C.J. was one of the five freshmen elevated to the varsity baseball team and inserted into the starting lineup almost immediately. Before long, his name would be penciled in as the leadoff man and second baseman, a position he wouldn't vacate until graduation. C.J. was born to be a leadoff hitter. He had a good eye and quality bat, a combination that would produce record on-base percentages and stamp his name onto the state record books for stolen bases and runs. Leading off a game, if C.J. got on base, the other team knew what would happen next. Homer was winning 1-0 before you could blink. Generally, C.J. would steal second (and sometimes third) before being brought home by Ryan Thurston or Dale Cornstubble. "If C.J. didn't get on [in the first inning], it was kind of like, 'Oh man.' That's a lot of pressure," Salow said.

C.J. didn't mind pressure. A starting guard on the basketball team and quarterback/receiver on the football team, C.J. wouldn't know what to do if he didn't have sports. Never a big kid, he made up for size with guts rarely seen from a teenage athlete. Always going 100 miles per hour, the head-first slider on the base paths usually had his uniform completely covered in dirt by the second inning. Growing up with an intense father/coach prepared him well for the pressures that came with the winning streak and national attention. But C.J. didn't spend much time thinking about all the hoopla. As he said, "I just wanted to play baseball."

In Finch's first three years of high-school ball, Homer rarely played in close games, so there weren't tons of high-pressure situations. When there were, Homer's players usually came through. But for a few hours in the state title game against Nouvel, the Trojans were human. They made mistakes. They were

C.J. FINCH MAKES A DIVING TAG OUT.
PHOTO BY KEVIN FOWLER, COURTESY OF THE LANSING STATE JOURNAL.

on the wrong side of bad breaks. And in the end, the scoreboard didn't look familiar. Perhaps the game's biggest play was when Nouvel's Matt Kretz hit a two-run bloop single over Finch's head at second base. The hit came with two outs, giving the Panthers the decisive two-run advantage in their seven-run fourth inning. Those who were in attendance still don't know how the ball rose over Finch's glove. It appeared as if the sure-handed second baseman had it all the way. But when Finch took one errant step in, the ball had enough spin to get just over his outstretched arm.

"It's still with me," Finch said well after the fact. "I'll never forget those plays. Looking back, I kind of had the approach,

'You can't do anything about it now.' You need to get over it. Breaks didn't happen the way we wanted it to. It was a heart-breaker. I don't really like to go back and think about it."

C.J. showed his character and toughness by answering every reporter's question after the tough loss. It was an impressive showing for a young man who had just endured the most gut-wrenching loss of his young career. But then again, Finch had been through much more trying times before. After all, this was a kid who had to live with his father trying to oust his coach.

>>><<<

He might not have thought about it often, but Salow had a great deal of respect for the way in which C.J. Finch dealt with the uncomfortable situation that surrounded his father. C.J. was nothing if not tough, and he really displayed that trait during his baseball career. After the arbitration was over and it was decided that Salow would keep his job, he and C.J. had a sit-down to hash out everything before the season started. Neither person involved remembers much about the meeting, except to say that everything went fine and both agreed it would be best to just focus on the upcoming baseball season. "We said no hard feelings," C.J. recalls. "I have a lot of respect for coach. He's a great guy. One of the nicest guys I know."

C.J. was not as outspoken as his father, but he was equally honest. His thoughts about liking and respecting Salow were absolutely true. But he also had other feelings that never made it into newspapers or television features. They might've never even been uttered to trusted teammates on long bus rides. C.J. liked playing for Scott Salow; that cannot be understated. He liked winning and that's all he did under Salow's leadership. More than that, though, C.J. had a fierce loyalty to his father: a trust that could never be matched.

Chuck Finch once said, "C.J. plays baseball and he studies." It was Chuck's way of saying there was no need for his son to worry about what was going on in his workplace, where as an influential member of the teachers' association, he felt obligated to prevent Salow from being head baseball coach and middle-school principal. To Chuck's credit, he objected to something he thought was wrong, but he didn't bring his son into the equation. There was never any family meeting where Chuck told C.J. to start a revolt against Salow. In Chuck's mind this was a matter that would be settled between adults and there was no benefit in dragging C.J. into the mix. That being said, there's no question where C.J.'s loyalty was. It was in the man he said "taught him everything about the game of baseball." C.J. was referring to his father, Chuck Finch.

True to form as the ultimate team player, C.J. never caused any dissent between players on Homer, despite his unique position as son of the man who wanted the head-coaching job. Make no mistake, the spunky dark-haired young man who could run like crazy had strong feelings about the controversy involving Homer baseball. C.J. didn't believe Salow should've been ousted. Instead, he was proud of his father for taking a stand. For several years as the head of Homer's teachers union, Chuck had

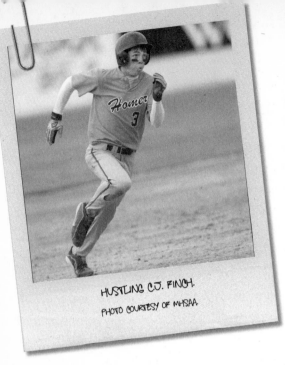

HUSTLING C.J. FINCH.
PHOTO COURTESY OF MHSAA.

been an outspoken man, unafraid to oppose the majority to stand up for his principles. C.J. had seen it many times over. To C.J., this was just another example of dad not taking any crap. Except even C.J. had to admit this was a bit unusual, considering his team was involved.

"He was just looking to do what was best for us," C.J. said about Chuck. "Him and Tom Sharpley, they taught us what we knew about the game [from pre-high-school teams]. We had all of our coaching. We knew the game of baseball; it was just a matter of going out and doing it. You ask any of those guys and they'll tell you we learned most of our stuff from [Chuck and Sharpley]. They knew where the coaching came from."

C.J. said that Salow was a great manager of the game but he couldn't compare with Chuck in terms of baseball fundamentals. "When it comes down to baseball intelligence, we know who we are listening to and that was my dad," he said. "Whenever somebody was having trouble hitting, they'd call my dad and he'd come down and have a look at their swing.

He'd always come down and work with us on our hitting after practice. When it came down to knowledge of the game, hitting-wise, knowing the particulars, knowing throwing motions and pitching motions, we already knew that. [Salow] didn't teach us that because we already knew that coming in."

As for Salow's bunting and hustling style of baseball, C.J. agreed wholeheartedly with that approach. Having grown up around the Homer baseball program — Chuck was a J.V. coach for several years — that method of baseball was pretty well ingrained in C.J.'s brain by the time he entered high school. Furthermore, C.J. said that Chuck didn't make a habit of criticizing Salow's in-game decisions around the house, even after the bitter controversy ended poorly for his father.

"Most of the games, we killed teams," C.J. said, "and Coach Salow is strategically solid. As players we performed. I knew we were going to win either way [whoever was coach]. When it comes to hustling on and off the field and small ball, their styles are similar."

Salow's style was perfect for a player like C.J. Finch. As a small but athletic kid, C.J. was able to show off his talents because Salow always had him stealing bases and taking the extra base on a hit to the outfield. The hustling part was right up C.J.'s alley too. Hardly a home-run hitter, C.J. was going to be noticed by the little things he did. And that's how Salow loved to play. If C.J. got on base, which he so often did, he'd look across the diamond to invariably see Salow flash the steal sign. Almost without fail, C.J. would be passing Salow by at his third-base coaching box shortly after with a timely run for the Trojans. C.J. was sharp enough to understand all that. He was also bright enough to know that outwardly questioning his coach would have zero positive consequences. Instead, the gritty second baseman who grew up on a baseball diamond blended in like any other player on the team. But both because of talent and his strange off-the-field situation, C.J. was no ordinary player.

While C.J. never posed problems for Salow, the coach did have this to say about his leadoff hitter. "In a year, C.J. will be playing college baseball somewhere and life will be back to normal," Salow said after Finch's junior season, which ended in the championship-game loss to Nouvel. "I can't wait for that. I mean, I love C.J., but I'm ready for him to graduate just so his dad is off my back a little bit."

Chuck Finch and Tom Sharpley coached several of the players who went on to star for Homer High when the boys were aged 11-15. Josh Collmenter, Dan Holcomb, Dusty Compton, and C.J., of course, were among the group that played on summer teams based in Marshall, a town about 15 minutes north of Homer. They were originally called the Marshall Battle Kids (a play on words of the Midwest League team in Battle Creek, then known as the Michigan Battle Cats) before becoming the Mid-Michigan Tigers. Years before anyone thought about national win streaks or state championships, Sharpley and Finch enthusiastically taught the boys fundamentals and a love for baseball while also putting tons of miles on their cars driving to tournaments all over the Midwest. When most of the kids were in sixth grade, Sharpley and Finch took them on a Far East excursion to a world tournament in Japan. Always in search of good competition, the boys went to Nashville, Tenn., the following year. "I don't think we thought about what it was going to mean down the road," Sharpley said. "Josh, Dusty, C.J., and Dan were all real good players when they were young. They had committed parents that were willing to sacrifice and travel."

Sharpley and Finch remain friends to this day. "The biggest thing about Chuck is he's very passionate, very intense," said Sharpley, whose oldest son Evan went on to play quarterback at the University of Notre Dame. "We were probably hardest on our own kids. He'd stay after it with them. The biggest thing is commitment. Being there in the morning when the sun comes up either way."

After the arbitration case, as lives eased back into normality, the team went about its business of being teenagers and playing baseball in the 2005 season, the junior seasons for most of the boys. C.J. was still one of the guys, but there was one subject that remained hidden in a lock box. "We never really talked about it," Holcomb said of the Salow-Chuck Finch issue. "We knew C.J. was in a tough spot. We shied away from it. When we played or worked out, everything was focused on baseball." For C.J. too, concentrating on sports and school was how he stayed sane through the uneasy times. One particularly tough evening for C.J. was the board meeting in the packed gymnasium where people showed their near-unanimous support for Salow. It was the night where Salow had intended to resign from the principal post but instead the school board voted to keep him as both principal and baseball coach. Far behind the commotion near the podium, C.J. Finch stood back and listened as town members, teachers, players past and present supported Salow. To a teenage boy, it sounded like a public ripping of his role model and loving father.

"It was a little awkward," C.J. said. "A few people spoke out for Mr. Salow; they were players in the past who really shouldn't have been on the field. I didn't respect some of the people. I just wanted to play ball. I remember one person, it took a lot for me not to stand up, a former player … and he said some things about my dad and I just bit my tongue. Deep down I wanted to blast him."

>>><<<

Once the hazy dust from the arbitration had settled, Chuck Finch continued on with his role in the HEA, a teacher at the school and an assistant coach for the J.V. baseball and football teams. In an attempt to extend the proverbial olive branch, Salow invited Finch to attend some varsity practices and help the kids during drill work. There were never any incidents between the two men as both went about their business and did what they could to make Homer better. On game days, Chuck was back in the stands rooting loudly for C.J. and his alma mater.

Of course, Chuck was there with his family at C.O. Brown Stadium when the record streak was broken as their proud village watched the unthinkable. "For C.J., I was probably most proud with how he handled losing that championship game," Chuck said shortly after the loss. "It's easy to be fired up and competitive when things go your way. They didn't pout, they shook hands, and they didn't sulk. I was really proud of the way they handled that. It was a bummer but they handled it well. They're hungry. They feel they should have won that. Next year, they want to win it again and anything short of that will be a disappointment."

Josh Collmenter, who was now on his way toward making the Louisville Slugger Freshman All-American team at Central Michigan, had a unique perspective on Homer's soap opera. In high school, Collmenter dated Christina Finch, C.J.'s older sister and a quality athlete herself. Collmenter, who was a regular at the Finch house, recalled conversations with Christina regarding the sticky situation.

"I didn't really talk to C.J. a whole lot, but I'm sure it was a weird position for him," Collmenter said. "I know it was rough for Christina and we talked about it a few times. I don't think anyone would've had a problem if Mr. Finch was our coach, a lot of guys played for him when they were younger in football or with some summer baseball teams. But I think everyone was so supportive of us keeping the same group together and the same philosophy. I don't think there was a lot of bitterness because to have that job at that moment was a big opportunity for anyone, so [Chuck] was going to pursue it on a personal level."

Meanwhile, the notoriety that the Trojans had enjoyed for several months was gone. Along the way, Homer and its coaches were put on a stage for observers everywhere to witness the way the Trojans' played ball. With all the television features from ESPN and local stations, and the big games Homer played in, its seven-second rule and ferocious foul-ball chasing were on full display. Most of Homer's tactics were pleasing to the general viewing public. It was fun to see kids hustle like hell and play good baseball, too. Seeing that and more garnered Salow his share of fans, inside Homer and out. One of them was John Johnson, the MH-SAA's veteran director of communications.

DAN HOLCOMB REARS BACK.
PHOTO BY JOHN GRAP, COURTESY OF THE BATTLE CREEK ENQUIRER

"He's the kind of coach I would want my kids to play for, and I don't say that very often," Johnson gushed. "I only have three or four such coaches. But Scott Salow would be in that group. He managed to keep it all in perspective, managed to keep his grace, managed to lead in different ways, but always by example. The important things he taught were fundamentals and fun. I didn't see anything that wasn't fundamentally sound. Nothing, not even warm-ups, was done haphazard. Their fundamentals were phenomenal. Not a single person in uniform had their perspective out of whack. All I saw was 'Yes sir, no sir,' to the coach. The respect kids and adults alike had for this coach was remarkable."

The offseason between 2005 and 2006 was fairly uneventful. The four-way circle drive in downtown Homer was renamed Championship Drive, with Scott and Tom Salow posing for pictures in the *Index*. Several players and Salow garnered more postseason awards but after a few months, life was back to normal in the little village. Dan Holcomb, having already accepted a scholarship offer from the University of Evansville (Ind.) of the Missouri Valley Conference, decided not to play basketball or football so as to concentrate solely on baseball.

This caused a bit of a stir at school, where the basketball and football coaches were counting on Holcomb being an important member of their teams. In hoops, the 6-foot-3 Holcomb was a starting shooting guard. In football, he was the returning starting quarterback. But Holcomb, who would later serve as the class valedictorian, was steadfast in his decision. Despite the pleadings of friends, coaches, and even his father, who was a former college football player, Dan stuck to his decision. Even Scott Salow told Holcomb he should play the other sports — this was his last chance to play under the Friday night lights.

"It was extremely tough because all the coaches were extremely good to me," Holcomb said. "I was really close to all of them; most of them were teachers at the school. To go away from them was tough. But football and basketball weren't my best sports. In basketball, I was a 6-3 kid who played two-guard and couldn't shoot very well, I was slow and I couldn't jump very much."

Football was a little tougher to give up for Holcomb. His father Brent and his uncles were all former football players. Dan still supported his friends and his school, and he could be found sitting in the student section during home football games. C.J. Finch took over the quarterbacking duties in Holcomb's place and fellow baseball player Kyle Meeks was an All-Area defensive back. With Holcomb watching from the stands, Homer had its best football season in years, advancing to the second round of the state playoffs.

>>><<<

While Holcomb's former teammates in basketball and football were representing their school, the talented pitcher was spending his time in Grand Rapids working with professional coaches and trying to expand his mound repertoire.

Holcomb had a driving buddy for all those trips back and forth from Grand Rapids, which was about 100 miles each way. Catcher Dale Cornstubble, who was always a one-sport guy, was training with Holcomb at the Diamonds Sports Training Facility. While there was snow on the ground and baseball seemed a million miles away for most high schoolers in Michigan, Holcomb and Cornstubble were working on techniques and drills to improve themselves. They were also developing an inseparable pitcher-catcher bond that went beyond the diamond.

On dozens of occasions over three-plus years, Holcomb and Cornstubble made the trek to the Diamond Sports complex. In the beginning, the boys' fathers would drive Dale and Dan northwest, often in Dale Sr.'s 1998 Ford Explorer or wife Julie's 2000 Chevrolet Impala. When Brent Holcomb drove, the boys would pack into the back of his Ford F-150. Baseball talk flowed freely as the teenagers and their fathers found a way to kill nearly four hours roundtrip on the road. "Sometimes we would get up there three times a week," Dale Cornstubble said.

The Diamonds training facility provided both players with coaching and resources simply not available in Homer. Diamonds boasts more than 22,000 square feet of turf, nine batting cages, clay and portable pitching mounds, video training, and every other modern amenity to help a young baseball player develop. Holcomb and Cornstubble scheduled sessions with owner Bill Peterson and his staff, which included former Baltimore Orioles manager Phil Regan, Cincinnati Reds scout Rick Sellers, former major-league draft pick Kevin Baker, and Casey Fisk, son of Hall of Fame catcher Carlton Fisk. "I needed to get out and go somewhere where people were experienced and involved in the game," Cornstubble said.

Holcomb added: "When you're around baseball that much, you hear the way [the instructors] talked about it and acted, it helped our learning curve on the game so much. It was a blast; some of our best times were up there. Everybody was extremely serious about baseball, but it was still a lighthearted atmosphere."

Holcomb received pitching lessons from Regan, an Otsego, Michigan native who spent 13 seasons in the majors, earning 96 MLB wins along with the nickname "The Vulture." It was eye-opening knowledge for Holcomb, who'd spent his heretofore baseball career rearing back and throwing fastballs past overmatched high-school hitters. "I had never had a pitching coach before," Holcomb said. "It helped with the mechanics of pitching, and how to correct mechanics in the middle of a game. Being able to pick up little things about the game, you just feel a lot more comfortable out on the field after you work out with those guys."

Peterson first saw Holcomb at a club team tryout at Eastern Michigan University after Dan's freshman year. He was throwing 83-84 miles per hour, and with a big, strong frame, Dan's potential was obvious. "Dan's hard work combined with Phil's tutelage helped Dan turn the corner," Peterson said. "The biggest progress he made was his ability to throw his curveball for a strike. And he worked hard on his changeup, giving him three pitches that he could throw at any time."

Cornstubble, meanwhile, was learning new techniques on hitting and catching. He also went from being a scrawny little kid to impressive stature, thanks to working religiously with Casey Fisk, the Diamonds' strength-training coach. Dale was widely being considered the best catching prospect in Michigan.

"Dale was flat out the best catch-and-throw guy I've ever seen at the high school level," Peterson said. "He did things you just don't see from a 17- or 18-year-old player. You could tell immediately that he was special." Brett Allman, the Quincy coach who faced Homer twice each year in conference play, thought Cornstubble was the team's "X" factor in terms of turning a very good team into a great one.

"Cornstubble was impressive," Allman said. "As good as their pitching was, if you had someone behind the plate you can steal on, maybe you can manufacture a run here and there. But you had to have two or three hits in an inning to get a run across, and a lot of times you only had that many [hits] in the game. Their pitching was awful good but when you combine that with the catching behind the plate, it makes it so tough. They fed off Dale; he was one of their emotional leaders."

Holcomb and Cornstubble were something of an odd couple. Holcomb, son of the superintendent, and Cornstubble, son of a school custodian, certainly had different upbringings. The Cornstubbles weren't living in poverty, but they didn't have a lot either. After Dale started as a freshman on the varsity, his father, Dale Sr., bought his son a $3,000 Jason Giambi Backyard Package, a batting cage that was set up behind the family's garage. This was no small purchase for the family.

"I was 15 and supposed to be getting my license soon, but I never did because I got a batting cage," Cornstubble says with a laugh. "No car for me until I was 17." Cornstubble made the most of his new toy, and then some. The summer after he got the cage, Dusty Compton was living at the Cornstubbles' home and the two boys spent countless hours in the cage. They would crank the pitching machine as high as it would go just to see if they could get their bats around on the speedy balls.

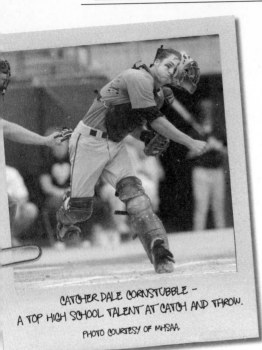

CATCHER DALE CORNSTUBBLE –
A TOP HIGH SCHOOL TALENT AT CATCH AND THROW.
PHOTO COURTESY OF MHSAA

When Dale was sick of hitting, he'd adjust the pitching arm downward, put on his catching gear, and work for hours on blocking balls in the dirt (or cement, as it were).

Backyard practice at Dale's didn't end when the weather turned chilly either. "Me and Compton were crazy. We used to go out there with stocking caps on and three sweatshirts and we'd go hit. That's just what we lived for."

After the boys turned 16, they would often travel to Grand Rapids by themselves in Alice Holcomb's Infinity. At first, Dan preferred rap music while Dale liked his rock and country. "By the end, all I listened to was rock and country after hanging out with him," Holcomb said. Even when they were in Homer, Holcomb and Cornstubble were spending more and more time together. When they weren't playing baseball, they were hunting deer, pheasants, or squirrels. Or fishing or playing video games. Cornstubble bought the 2K3 Baseball for his Microsoft XBox, and the friends would make teams and play entire seasons on the video system.

Despite Dan's status as son of the superintendent, that fact never got in the way of friendship. "Dan was never the kid to brag about all that stuff, not even a little bit," Dale said.

The odd couple formed a dynamic duo at 60 feet, 6 inches away from each other on a baseball diamond. The two players knew each other's strengths and weaknesses so well, it was like having another coach in between the lines. No topic, good or bad, was out of bounds. "If he called a pitch that I didn't want to throw, he'd get mad at me," Dan said. "Or if something would happen [negatively], I'd blame it on him. He'd come out to the mound and start yelling at me and I'd start yelling at him. Everyone thought it was just like a boyfriend-girlfriend fight or a husband-wife fight so we got razzed about that."

As Holcomb and Cornstubble worked on their individual games, Homer's baseball team was getting better in the process. With every nugget of instruction from the pros at Diamonds, the two players were learning things that would help the Trojans once the high school season started. Every time Holcomb or Cornstubble got better, so did the Homer Trojans. Holcomb was throwing in the high 80s and adding complementary pitches. Cornstubble, like his teammate, chose to end the recruiting process early and committed to Central Michigan where he would rejoin Josh Collmenter. All in all, Homer's odd couple was primed for huge senior years. That should've been a scary thought for future opponents.

Coach Salow's trophy case.
Photo by Doug Allen.

Expectations & Challenges

When practice began in the spring of 2006, the Trojans knew this year was about finishing it right. It was about finishing their careers with another state title and making sure it didn't slip away like the championship game from the year before. As 12 seniors prepared for their last season of high-school baseball together, winning the whole thing would be the only acceptable outcome. Homer would be playing this season in Division 4, the smallest classification for baseball in the state. The perception was that Homer would simply sprint through the D4 competition, that this year's playoffs wouldn't be fun for anyone. Nothing could've been further from the truth.

Only rightfielder Brandon Gibson had graduated from last year's starting lineup. The remaining eight positions, including two fantastic pitchers in Holcomb and Compton, returned in '06 for Homer. After seeing a few candidates compete for the starting right-field spot, Salow settled on sophomore Austin Rinard, a talented and impressively built young athlete. Rinard would bat low in the order, as Salow hoped to shield him from big-pressure situations. There was plenty of pressure on the other players, specifically Homer's returning eight senior starters, who desperately wanted to prove they could win a championship without Collmenter and Powers.

Expectations were through the roof. "Anytime you return five All-Staters and eight starters, you are expected to win every game and win a state championship," Salow said before the season. "I think we certainly are capable of winning a state championship, but people think because we are Division 4 all we have to do is show up. I guarantee you it won't be that easy, but certainly we have a goal of getting to the championship game at Battle Creek."

With Holcomb on the mound, Homer opened up its 2006 season with an 11-2 victory over Marshall on a ridiculously cold and windy March day. Homer's win streak now stood at one. "It was a typical March baseball game in Michigan," Salow said. "We put 11 runs on the board, but we didn't have to do much to get it. We got a lot of walks, but we took advantage of them somewhat. I think we left too many runners on base. We got 11 runs, but we should've had 20." Holcomb tossed five innings to keep his personal win streak alive, and Compton came on in relief for the final two innings of work. A full season lay ahead, and the Trojans were ready to build a new streak.

The weather stayed cold, but the victories continued to pile up. Homer's senior-laden team was cruising through its regular season competition when another big record was suddenly in its midst. Dan Holcomb, who lost one game during his freshman year, hadn't lost a decision since. When Holcomb took the mound on April 27, he was one triumph away from setting the all-time state record for consecutive victories. As if there were any doubt in the outcome, the Trojans smoked Hudson High 10-0 in five innings for Holcomb's 32nd straight win. It

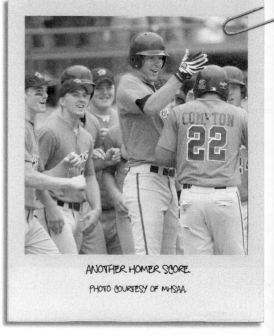

ANOTHER HOMER SCORE.
PHOTO COURTESY OF MHSAA.

broke the record of 31 straight wins by Doug Vanderwall of Grand Haven High School, who played from 1959-61. Lost in the achievement was the fact that Hudson marked Holcomb's second straight no-hitter and his third of the season. None of the games had lasted a full seven innings because of Homer's dominance.

"It really is a tribute to the team," Holcomb told the *Index*. "If we hadn't lost in the finals last year, Dusty probably would have beaten me to the record. Looking at the schedule, we knew all our games are winnable so I knew it was possible."

Salow added: "When Danny first started throwing as a freshman we knew he had potential because of his size and live arm. But just like winning 75 games in a row as a team, you certainly don't think a pitcher is going to win 32 straight times."

Homer was 14-0 and looking as unbeatable as ever.

>>><<<

During the season, Salow got a phone call from Lansing, asking if Homer would be interested in playing in the prestigious Diamond Classic Tournament. The tournament, which was in its 45th year, was a big deal in the Lansing area. It was played at Oldsmobile Park, home of the minor-league Lansing Lugnuts, and there was a great deal of civic pride involved in the event.

Part of that civic pride was the belief of Lansing's baseball community that the tournament be comprised of only local teams. While Homer is only about 60 miles from Lansing, it was outside of the area's consciousness. Lansing has several excellent baseball programs in the area — most notably in neighboring suburbs — and the locals wanted it to remain *their* event. A committee of about six men chooses the Diamond Classic's field each year. It's generally composed of the 10 best teams in the mid-Michigan area. When the subject was broached of including Homer in the 2006 field, it was met with some skepticism. "It certainly brought a lot of enthusiasm to the event, but there were some in the area that felt jilted because it's an area event," said Geoff Kimmerly, the *Lansing State Journal*'s prep sports editor. "It's a Lansing-area tournament, and Homer is not a Lansing-area team." Homer was believed to be the first team in the tournament's 45-year history to be from outside the Lansing area.

Like so many community traditions in modern America, the Diamond Classic has changed some over the years. In the early years, the tournament was held at Municipal Park, a dirt-infield venue with wooden benches and a palpable old-time feel. Without much seating available in the bleachers, crowds used to line the fences back in the 1960s, with thousands on hand to watch baseball when it was indeed America's Pastime. That, of course, has changed. But even as cable television, the NFL, and the NBA have staked their claim on the short-attention-span generation, some things have remained part of a community. "For baseball people in the area, I think it's still a big deal," Kimmerly said of the DC. "The thing's got tradition."

Part of the uniqueness of the Diamond Classic is its timing. While most high-school tournaments are over one weekend during the regular season, the DC overlaps two weeks and into the beginning of the state playoffs. Three days before the district playoffs began, the Trojans made their Diamond Classic debut against a 23-win, Division 2 Fowlerville team.

Homer, making its first ever DC appearance, and Fowlerville, playing in its first DC event since 1996, took the field on a Wednesday night in June. Much of the crowd was from Homer, of course. People used to joke the team could play games out of state and they'd still travel to see their boys. Gale Smith, the Main Street barber, once said village residents such as him who worked until 5 or 5:30 p.m. during the week could only see an inning or two of most home games because the mercy-rule blowouts usually ended before 6. Now, fans like Smith made sure to skip out of work early to see their boys on the big stage.

The setting at Oldsmobile Park was special, even for players who'd traveled all over during summer tournaments and who had played in state title games at C.O. Brown Stadium in Battle Creek. The park, which has retained the name even since the car company folded, was built in 1996 as a Midwest League affiliate for the Kansas City Royals and has since been home to Chicago Cubs and Toronto Blue Jays farm teams. The gorgeous stadium is located smack in the middle of downtown Lansing, just down the street from the state Capitol. Carlos Beltran and Carlos Zambrano played home games here, and dozens of others have made the major leagues after playing in Lansing. With a big scoreboard in the outfield and a digital screen that displays the radar-gun results on every pitch, this was not a normal high-school venue.

The lead to Kimmerly's story in the *Lansing State Journal* the day after Homer dismantled Fowlerville 10-0 in the first round of the Diamond Classic read: "Homer wasted all of 16 pitches Wednesday before showing why it has created a buzz in mid-Michigan since being selected for the 45th Diamond Classic last week. On the 17th pitch the Trojans got a double play that ended Fowlerville's only sniff of a scoring opportunity." Dusty Compton was dominant on the mound for Homer, as 1,163 fans watched the two-game session. The Trojans scored six runs in the third inning, and with Compton mowing down Fowlerville's hitters, the game ended 10-0 after five innings. "We just haven't faced anything like that before," Fowlerville's Justin Stawara told the *State Journal*.

Playing a regular-season game just days before a double-header to open the playoffs isn't ideal, but it hardly mattered. Homer slaughtered lowly Big Eight representative Concord and North Adams Jerome by a combined score of 30-0 to claim a sleeper of a Division 4 district title. What for most teams would've been cause for celebration was barely noticed when senior shortstop Ryan Thurston hit three home runs, including two grand slams with 12 RBI, *and* pitched a no-hitter. Thurston, who improved his record to 6-0, pitched because Compton threw against Fowlerville and Salow knew his third hurler would be just fine against the weaker competition. "I hit at my house before the game and I wasn't hitting that great," Thurston told the *Index*. "I hit some more at batting practice, but still didn't feel real good. But once the game started, I got zoned in."

With just one day off after the district games, the Trojans traveled back to Lansing to face Okemos High in a Diamond Classic semifinal. Facing Fowlerville had

RYAN THURSTON CAME UP BIG,
AND WAS NAMED CO-MVP OF THE STATE TOURNAMENT.
PHOTO COURTESY OF MHSAA.

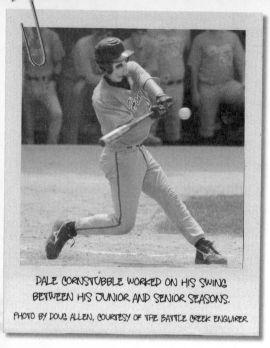

DALE CORNSTUBBLE WORKED ON HIS SWING BETWEEN HIS JUNIOR AND SENIOR SEASONS.

PHOTO BY DOUG ALLEN, COURTESY OF THE BATTLE CREEK ENQUIRER

been one thing, but the Okemos Chieftains were something completely different. Okemos, a Division 1 school with an enrollment of around 1,400, fancies an impressive athletic portfolio. Though this wasn't one of Okemos' better baseball teams, it still would finish the year 29-8, and it certainly qualified as one of Homer's biggest challenges.

Okemos, a charming community on the outskirts of Lansing, had never won the Diamond Classic. Although this game against Homer was just a semifinal, a victory for the Chieftains would be as satisfying as a title. Like most teams that played Homer over the past few years, Okemos was sick and tired of hearing about how great the boys in orange were. Unlike most teams that played Homer, the Chieftains came out and did something about it on the field.

By the bottom of the fifth inning, Okemos led 4-2 as 2,217 fans watched the Chieftains outplay Homer. (In recent years, the Diamond Classic was averaging about 800 fans per day). In the fifth, the Trojans began to rally. A single by Dale Cornstubble scored C.J. Finch to cut Homer's deficit to 4-3.

After Dusty Compton flied out, Dan Holcomb and Cody Collmenter walked to load the bases.

Down at the third-base coaching box, Salow flashed the "catcher pickoff" sign to Collmenter. Even with two outs, Salow figured the play was worth a shot. On the first pitch to Brock Winchell, Collmenter strayed off first base and then fell down like he'd been pushed from behind. As it always did, the play caused the opposing catcher to fire the ball toward first. When Okemos' catcher threw, Cornstubble broke for home plate. Okemos' first baseman caught the ball but then fired wildly to second, allowing Cornstubble and Holcomb to score. Just like that, Homer had a 5-4 lead without the benefit of a two-out hit. Okemos' fans stared in silence, wondering how Collmenter had fallen down off of first and how their team wasn't able to take advantage. The large contingent of Homer fans knew better; they'd seen the play work time after time, most notably to win the 2004 Division 3 semifinal against Muskegon Oakridge.

Homer scored four more runs in the sixth inning to take a 9-4 lead. With Okemos down to its final out in the seventh, a foul pop was hit toward Homer's dugout. It looked like a routine foul ball until Cornstubble appeared out of nowhere to make a spectacular diving catch into the dugout for the game-winner. The image of Cornstubble holding the ball up after catching it, along with Tom Salow leaping out of the dugout and several Homer reserves going nuts, would later appear in the *Detroit News*. "I don't think we have to prove anything, but to come in here and go up against a school four times our size in enemy territory says a lot about our kids," Salow told the *Index*'s Mike Warner. "We had every chance to fold but we didn't. These kids have shown time and time again they have the hearts of champions."

That might be true, but the Trojans weren't Diamond Classic champions yet. For that to happen, Homer would have to face the best Lansing's area had to offer. That would be the Grand Ledge Comets, winners of a record 18 Diamond Classic titles. No one was close when it came to Lansing area baseball supremacy, as evidenced by the next closest school (Lansing Everett, Magic Johnson's alma mater, has seven DC titles). Grand Ledge was coached by the legendary Pat O'Keefe, who would later join Blissfield's Larry Tuttle as the only members of Michigan's 900-win club. Grand Ledge was often accused of being arrogant, but that's what happens when you're always on top. The Comets would just say they're confident. Either way, Grand Ledge was generally the envy of area high schools when it came to baseball.

The weekend before the DC semifinals, Grand Ledge had been stunned by Battle Creek Central in the Division 1 districts. Battle Creek Central, a baseball doormat, had no business beating Grand Ledge, but it did, sending Grand Ledge to end its season at Oldsmobile Park.

Grand Ledge, wearing its patented blue and yellow pinwheel hats, represented baseball's bluebloods. Homer, with all of its recent success and glory, was the new team invited to sit at the big boys' royal table. Even though Homer wasn't necessarily playing well, the Trojans were handily defeating Grand Ledge through five innings. Holcomb didn't have his best command but he managed to pitch out of numerous jams. Homer's defense wasn't great either, yet the Trojans led 6-1 after six innings as the energized ballpark looked upon the strange site of Grand Ledge being tossed aside like just another middling opponent.

As Homer's raucous crowd awaited its latest big triumph, Holcomb ran into trouble in the seventh. He walked the first batter, gave up a single, and then walked another. An RBI single made the score 6-2, and Holcomb was replaced by Compton. Grand Ledge hit a sacrifice fly to narrow the score to 6-3 with one out and two runners on base. The stage was set for Grand Ledge's Trent Pohl and the most dramatic Diamond Classic moment in more than 20 years. Needing just two outs for the DC championship, Compton hung a slider to Pohl, who promptly jacked the ball over the left-field fence for a three-run homer, tying the score at 6. The park erupted, a familiar sound for Homer, except its fans weren't the ones making noise. The Lansing Lugnuts had a game later that night, and several players and the coaching staff sat behind the backstop watching every pitch intently.

Emotionally exhausted, Homer gave up a run in the eighth inning and lost 7-6. Grand Ledge's season ended at 32-5 with its 19th Diamond Classic title. Homer's season was still alive, but the 33-1 Trojans were shell-shocked. The strange thing was how similar the loss was to Homer's last defeat, also 7-6, and also because it surrendered a five-run inning. This wasn't for the state title but it hurt all the same. The next day's *Lansing State Journal* had a huge picture of Grand Ledge celebrating, flanked by two stories about the game and the headline in bold type: "Instant Classic." For two decades, the defining moment of the Diamond Classic had been a famous home run in 1985 by Lansing Waverly's John Smoltz, who later starred for years as a pitcher for the Atlanta Braves. Now, Grand Ledge's Pohl gave the DC a new signature moment.

"Yeah, they've won a lot of games," Pohl told the *State Journal*. "But [hearing about it] gets old after awhile. They've got a good team. I figured people would probably root for Homer. Everybody hates us anyway."

Comets coach O'Keefe said: "I thought we were done for, especially after they brought their ace in. I thought that might be the end. Trent Pohl's home run might be in my history book as the best I've seen in the Diamond Classic."

Pohl shared the tournament's Most Valuable Player honors with Homer's Ryan Thurston, who had a two-run double in the title game.

State Journal sports columnist Todd Schulz opined that he'd been wrong in criticizing the inclusion of Homer in the Lansing tournament. "But everyone will talk about this one for years to come," Schulz wrote. "And that was the point of inviting Homer in the first place… Despite its Division 4 pedigree, Homer was hardly some cute, cuddly little team that could. The talented Trojans and what looked like their entire town strolled into the big stadium with a swagger befitting a team that had lost once in almost three seasons."

The *State Journal*'s Kimmerly, who also was against allowing a non-Lansing area school into the tournament, couldn't deny the excitement Homer brought. "It was insane," Kimmerly said later. "It was one of the top five high-school moments I've witnessed when Pohl hit that homer. It was good for the area and good for baseball. That was one of the most exciting things that's gone on around here in sports since I've been here [since 2000]."

Homer was now 108-2 in the last three years. The loss to Grand Ledge snapped a remarkable 98-game regular season winning streak. There'd be no time for sulking, though, with regionals three days away.

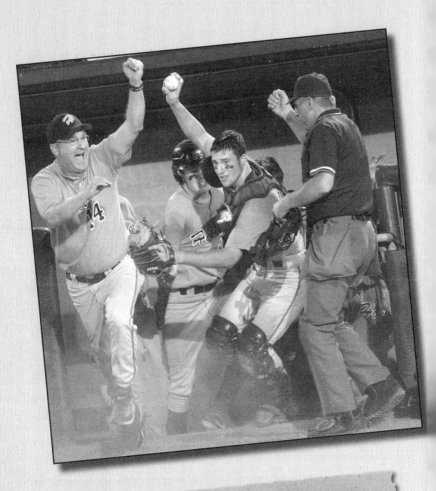

Tom Salow celebrates as Dale Cornstubble holds up the ball after making a spectacular catch and dive into the dugout to cap off the victory over Division 1 Okemos.
Photo by Dale G. Young, courtesy of the Detroit News.

The Dream Fulfilled

I t's unlikely that Homer's switch from Division 3 to D4 had any effect on its 2006 regular season. Except for a couple opponents, such as Division 2's Marshall, the Trojans were still playing much of the same schedule. Its foray into the Diamond Classic had been a major upgrade in competition that Homer hadn't been afforded in past years. So as the Trojans embarked on their quest for a second state title in the last three years, they seemed to have the same amount of readiness as prior seasons. It was in the playoffs, though, that Homer would learn about the differences between Divisions 3 and 4. What they would come to find out is that the high-quality teams were very similar in both divisions. It would be in the lower tier of schools that Homer would find itself outclassing the competition in the early rounds of playoff action.

Three days after the gut-wrenching loss to Grand Ledge, the Trojans took the field at home, as host of a Division 4 regional. Homer's historic group of seniors could now concentrate solely on its postseason road, which if it went the distance, would be five more games.

It took all of one batter for Homer to get back on track. C.J. Finch led off the regional semifinal with a solo home run, and the Trojans were off and running. Against overmatched Dansville, Ryan Thurston tossed a one-hit shutout with eight strikeouts, and Homer coasted to a 10-0 triumph. The easy win put Homer in the regional championship later that day against Pewamo-Westphalia for a berth in the Division 4 quarterfinals.

Dan Holcomb, who was the starting pitcher against Grand Ledge, was summoned on just two days of rest to throw against P-W. Holcomb showed nary a sign of fatigue, but the truth was, it probably didn't matter who pitched. When your offense scores 20 runs, Salow himself could've likely toed the rubber and came away with an easy victory. Holcomb struck out 13 batters while Finch, Cornstubble, and Holcomb homered as the Trojans won the regional championship, 20-0, in five innings.

"He handled himself well since a disappointing outing against Grand Ledge," Salow said of Holcomb. "We limited a good ballclub to just one hit." Holcomb improved to 13-0 on the year — Compton took the loss against Grand Ledge — and his state-record win streak now stood at 40 games.

Up next was a date with the Mount Pleasant Beal City Aggies at Dewitt High School (in the Lansing area) in a quarterfinal game. The winner would earn a trip to Battle Creek for the state semifinals. But before Homer got a chance to face Beal City, yet another red carpet was rolled out for the Trojans. This time the accolades were for Salow, who boasted a .901 winning percentage in his six years as head coach. While his team was preparing for the Aggies, Salow received word that he'd been named National Baseball Coach of the Year by the National High School Coaches Association. The group honors a national coach of the year in 20 different sports. "Being named coach of the year in the state of Michigan the last two years was plenty. But to be named in the same breath as some of the best coaches in the country, that says a lot about our team and our kids," Salow said. "It's good to get recognized for doing the right things on and off the field. I'm sure some day my children and grandchildren will appreciate it and that's good to know. But right now we're working on getting back to Battle Creek."

Homer and Beal City entered their quarterfinal game on opposite ends of the reputation spectrum. Homer (35-1) had been ranked first in Division 4 the entire season, taking that ranking into the playoffs. Beal City, at 29-6, was unranked and something of an unknown.

From the mere sight of watching Beal City go through its pregame warm-ups, the cocky side of Homer set in. "Look at these guys," they muttered to one another. "How are they in the quarterfinal?" Beal City's players were small in stature, its uniforms were awful plain, and its pregame infield and outfield practice was particularly underwhelming. The competitive edge that Homer took into its biggest games over the last three years was gone. The Trojans thought their third straight trip to Battle Creek was in the bag before the opening pitch was thrown.

>>><<<

Brett Bechtel had other ideas. What Beal City's diminutive right-handed pitcher lacked in size, he made up for in poise and moxie. Bechtel couldn't throw hard so he didn't try to. Instead, Beal City's ace, who entered the game 14-1, relied mostly on a pretty curveball and a sidearm slider to fool Homer's hitters. Beal City's other players, most of whom were as unintimidating as Bechtel, played the type of scrappy, fundamentally sound small-ball that the Trojans had turned into an art form.

With Dusty Compton on the mound, the Aggies scored first in the fourth inning on a suicide squeeze bunt. The Trojans immediately responded when Cornstubble hit a solo home run in the bottom half of the inning, tying the score 1-1. Homer then scored twice to take a 3-1 lead after an RBI single by Finch and a Beal City error. Beal City came right back in the sixth with three runs, two of them on bunts, to take a 4-3 advantage. When the Aggies scored again in the seventh, the Trojans were really in trouble. Only a throw by Homer's Austin Rinard from right field to home plate gunning down another Aggies potential run kept Homer within two at 5-3 as it sprinted into the dugout, three outs from an unthinkable elimination.

Homer's Kyle Meeks was hit by a pitch leading off the seventh, giving the Trojans a much-needed runner on base. However, two outs later, Meeks was still on base and the score remained 5-3. Just before the second out was made, Dale Cornstubble stood frozen on the on-deck circle. The reality of a career ending had sunk in for Homer's normally unflappable star catcher. "I went to go step on deck and I couldn't swallow," Cornstubble recalled. "I couldn't breath. I had this huge lump in my throat so I went in the dugout and had a huge glass of water." After Thurston made Homer's second out of the inning, Cornstubble walked slowly toward home plate. Upon reaching the batters box, he called timeout and shuffled toward Salow at the third-base coaching box.

"I was so nervous, my hands were shaking," he remembered. "I was in bad shape because everything we played for was on the line. So I asked coach if I should take a strike. He said, 'Hit the first one as hard and as far as you can.'"

Dale Cornstubble did just that. With the Homer Trojans one out from elimination, one out from an amazing three-year reign ending with just one state championship, the player regarded by many as the best catcher in Michigan, swung hard at the first pitch he saw. The player who spent hours upon hours with personal trainers in Grand Rapids and by himself in his backyard batting cage in Homer, connected perfectly on Bechtel's first offering. Cornstubble smashed the inside pitch toward left field. The only question was whether it would be a double or a home run. That was quickly answered when the ball narrowly cleared the left-field fence for a dramatic two-run homer, tying the score 5-5. As the ball disappeared, Homer first base coach Tom Salow erupted in celebration, as did the huge sea of orange in Homer's bleachers. "There was a lot of weight on my shoulders," Cornstubble said afterward. "I was just thinking there's no way it could end today."

Not to be outdone by his big brother, Scott Salow was hooting and hollering over at third base, too. "Because Dale had hit so well in the game, he hit a homer earlier and hit it hard the other time, I knew he'd hit it hard somewhere," Scott said. "But I never would've thought he'd hit it out for a two-run homer. You look at a lot of different plays over the last five years and that home run was one of the single most memorable moments. To be down to your last out, all of his buddies, 12 seniors, rooting for Dale and the game could've ended right there …"

Amazingly, the drama was just beginning. Holcomb, who had relieved Compton two innings earlier, retired Beal City 1-2-3 in the eighth. Homer now came to the plate in the bottom of the eighth, needing one run to add to its growing mystique.

Cody Collmenter hit a one-out single, but was still at first base with two outs. That's when the madness ensued. Rinard, Homer's lone underclassman starter, hit a single to shallow right field, and Collmenter attempted to go from first to third. Collmenter beat the throw from right field but Rinard temporarily lost his base-running mind. Perhaps in accordance with his lack of big-game experience, Rinard wasn't content with his single. The sophomore kept on running toward second base, and Beal City's infielders saw it all the way.

With Collmenter standing on third base, Beal City third baseman Matt Sharrar threw to shortstop Nick Steffke at second base for a sure out. The ball beat Rinard by several feet and he made an awkward but hard-nosed slide into Steffke. In what seemed like slow motion, the ball crawled out of Steffke's mitt and onto the dirt. Seeing this, Salow started jumping up and down at third base, signaling Collmenter to race for home.

He reached home plate without a throw as Steffke lay on the ground, writhing in pain as Homer pulled off yet another miraculous victory, this time 6-5 in eight innings. While Homer celebrated its third straight appearance in the state semifinals, Beal City coach Mike Allison sprinted toward the base umpire, claiming Rinard had slid illegally into his shortstop.

The next day in the *Mount Pleasant Morning Sun*, a newspaper that covers Beal City, the lead of the game story read: "The game was a classic. The ending was a calamity." Beal City, which had been one out away from a stunning upset, now had only the bitter taste of defeat in its mouth. "It looked to me like the kid came in shoulder down," Allison told the *Morning Sun*. "I know the ball was there and I was sure the runner was a dead duck. Most slides, you don't see a shortstop fall back three feet, but I don't know." Allison didn't find consolation in coming close. "We're not happy that we stuck within one run," he said, "we're devastated."

The feelings were quite different on Homer's side of the field. "I went from pissed off to happy pretty quick there," C.J. Finch said. "The emotions were outrageous. I was thinking this could be it and then Dale comes up and hits a bomb." Salow, though, was worried about his team's play. Similar to the previous year, the Trojans were not playing their best ball at season's end. Before Beal City, the Trojans had won their first four tournament games by a combined score of 60-0, but something still was awry. Maybe Homer had been lax after being unimpressed by Beal City in warmups. But it had almost cost the Trojans their season. Homer ended up winning despite committing four errors and generally looking out of whack for the entire afternoon. "I just had a different sense to the team when we came to the ballpark," Salow said afterward. "I don't know what to attribute that to. We just weren't ourselves. I didn't think we were that sharp anywhere. If things don't improve, we will exit this tournament on Friday [after their semifinal game]."

Homer's players were familiar with success, of course, over the past few seasons. Still, the celebration following the win over Beal City rivaled those after the national record and 2004 state championship. "I was pacing in the dugout, thinking, 'This can't be it,'" senior Brock Winchell said. "I think that was meant to happen to tell us that we're not all gods and we actually *can* lose. Before the game, [Beal City] looked like a Concord [a lower-tier Big Eight team]. They were small but they came out and beat us at our own game." Almost, anyway.

>>><<<

Upon leaving Dewitt, Homer's team bus made a detour on the way back to town. A former teacher at Homer, Rod Evans, who was also a baseball fan, rewarded the team with a steak dinner at Fire Mountain Grill in Lansing. "It was awesome," Cornstubble said. "We were getting refills of Dr Pepper, it was great. I slept really good that night."

One weekend remained for the special group of seniors on Homer. Win or lose, this was it. First up was Rochester Hills Lutheran Northwest (24-7). By now, Homer (36-1) learned that Division 4 wouldn't be a cakewalk. Beal City had demonstrated that.

With one, maybe two games left, Homer held one last practice on Thursday before the semifinal game. Since summer break had already begun, Salow held practices during the day when the weather was pleasant. Even on the last practice of the season, the Trojans worked on fundamentals like base running, bunting, and fielding grounders. Country music blared from a radio in the press box above the field, where a microphone sat next to the music box. Both Salows and assistant coach Mike Brooks shouted instructions and the boys ran around with the excitement of a team two wins away from glory. Then, all of a sudden, as the clock hit exactly noon, everybody stopped.

The national anthem played on the radio station, and Homer's players and coaches ceased what they were doing and spun around toward right field. Just like the perfect unity in which Homer executed the "catcher pickoff" play, every player and coach took his hat off and put it over his heart. There wasn't a flag in right field, but the players and coaches faced it anyway. For the entire anthem — which played promptly at noon every day on the country station — nobody moved or spoke. "At first Dusty just took his cap off," Cornstubble said, explaining the ritual's origins. "And then it just became tradition." It was another sign of Homer's team chemistry and their quirkiness, too. As soon as the anthem ended, practice resumed, and the Trojans continued on with their business of winning another state championship.

Dan Holcomb won his 41st straight decision in relief during the Beal City game. In Salow's two-ace system, Holcomb's arm was fresher than Compton's (who started against Beal

City), and therefore the Evansville-bound Holcomb was the starter against Lutheran Northwest. Holcomb's last-ever high-school start began ominously. After throwing seven consecutive balls to begin the Division 4 semifinal at C.O. Brown Stadium in Battle Creek, Holcomb's good friend and batterymate, Dale Cornstubble, trotted to the mound for a chat. "I got a little anxious out there and tried to throw a little too hard," Holcomb said. "Dale was a little mad. He said some things to get his point across."

As was often the case between the two friends, the motivation from Cornstubble did the trick. Holcomb settled down and promptly carved up Lutheran Northwest's hitters, one by one. The husky right-hander took a no-hitter into the sixth inning while striking out nine. Salow's fears were eased as Homer played flawless defense and got back to playing its game. The Trojans scored four runs on three hits in the second inning, helped largely by two Lutheran Northwest errors. By the fourth inning, Homer led 9-0 and a third straight trip to the championship game was just a few moments away.

Stepping into Homer's constantly rotating hero's role was senior third baseman/left fielder Brock Winchell. The seventh hitter in Homer's lineup, Winchell was always a tough out and a gritty player. Against Lutheran Northwest, he went 3-for-3 with two runs scored and an RBI as Homer cruised to a 9-1 win for Holcomb's 42nd straight victory. "Brock is a guy that just makes things happen," Salow said. "This is his time of year. He always comes up big at this time of year." Indeed, Winchell was Homer's version of Mr. October. Has anyone ever been dubbed Mr. June? Winchell was staking his claim on being an annual clutch performer. Two years prior, Winchell had scored the only run in the 1-0 epic quarterfinal victory over Blissfield. One year ago, he connected on the game-changing hit against Blissfield again in the quarters. Not bad for a seventh-place hitter.

The finality of it all was now tangible. One more game. That's all they had left. Homer's senior class had lost two games in three years and they'd won a state championship. If they could win one last game, they'd make it two state titles and leave an even bigger imprint on their legacy.

>>><<<

Homer had one more game, but it also had a big problem. Compton was nursing a sore right shoulder after falling over the mound during an infield drill in practice earlier in the week. The shoulder was hurting badly, made worse no doubt because of the tension pitchers inflict on their shoulder on a regular basis. Thurston and Finch had been excellent pitchers during the past few regular seasons, but neither had ever thrown in a high-pressure playoff game. This was no time for experimenting, either. So as Salow went to bed on the eve of the Division 4 state championship against Holton High (29-9), he had to at least consider the fact that Compton wouldn't be able to pitch. But in the back of Salow's mind, he knew there was no way to keep Dusty from exorcising the demons that still haunted the teenager a year after losing the state title game and national winning streak.

Thanks to its 7-2 victory over St. Joseph Lake Michigan Catholic, the Holton Red Devils would be Homer's title game opponent. A community of about 2,500 near Lake Michigan in the state's northwest region, Holton was an unfamiliar opponent for the Trojans. In the semifinal win over Lake Michigan Catholic, the Red Devils led 5-0 after two innings before coasting to victory. Holton's Ben Halbower tossed a complete game with seven strikeouts. The Red Devils had taken advantage of four Lake Michigan Catholic errors, a luxury that likely wouldn't be afforded against Homer.

Frankly, the nature of the Friday-Saturday finals weekend doesn't allow teams to know much about their title game opponent. You've got a few days to prepare for a semifinal foe, but once that game ends, it's usually 24 hours at the most until first pitch in the championship contest. Because of this and the fact Holton wasn't from its area, Homer didn't have much of a scouting report on the Red Devils. Salow and the boys weren't too concerned, though, because they knew preparing for Homer was also a daunting task for their opponent. In addition, the championship game appearance was a first for Holton, so the Red Devils had plenty on their plate as game time approached.

They say kids have short memories. That very well might be true, but it doesn't apply to Dusty Compton. Since taking the loss in the state championship game against Saginaw Nouvel in 2005, thus ending Homer's 75-game winning streak, Compton was hurting. Baseball and friends were essentially Compton's life, and he felt he let his buddies down during the game when Nouvel lit him up in that fourth inning when the Trojans gave up seven runs. Around school, Dusty wasn't himself as he walked down the hallways sulking. He'd plop down on a chair in Salow's office, only to tell the coach he still couldn't believe they hadn't won that game.

So it was fitting that almost exactly a year later, on the same mound of the same field, Compton had a chance for revenge. He would have seven innings to make sure he and his friends had a great final memory of their amazing high-school career. Man, did that shoulder hurt, but Dusty tried to block it out. He had no other choice.

"I thought I had a concussion at first," Compton said after he was drilled under the right cheek by a line drive from Holton's Cody Giddings. "I kind of blacked out when it hit me. But once I heard the crowd, I just wiped it all away."

It was the fifth inning and Compton had already allowed a two-out, two-run single that put Holton ahead, 2-1. Then came the line drive from Giddings that struck Compton's face as squarely as a round baseball can meet a human face. As Compton walked around the mound, trying to figure out which planet he was on, Homer's infielders and Salow came out to see if their pitcher was all right. Compton's black face paint was smeared when Cornstubble reached him at the mound. "I thought he should have caught it," Cornstubble told him. "He said, 'Let's get this next guy out.' It didn't faze him at all."

Compton retired the next batter on a fielder's choice and Homer was out of the inning. As the Trojans sprinted in for their at-bats in the bottom of the fifth inning, several problems existed. One, their pitcher who entered the game injured had just taken a Mike Tyson-like blow to the face, courtesy of a baseball. Secondly, the Trojans were losing 2-1 and had just three innings to change that. In the meantime, their legacy was on the line.

Homer immediately got to work in the fifth. Kyle Meeks was hit by a pitch, giving the Trojans a man on base with no outs. Finch then smacked a double to right-center, scoring Meeks and putting a runner in scoring position with no outs. With Homer's meat of the order up next, getting Finch home from second looked imminent. But it never happened. Thurston grounded out, Cornstubble walked, Compton struck out and Holcomb grounded out. Homer tied the game 2-2 but it also came up short with a golden opportunity to take the lead.

In the top of the sixth, Compton gave up a leadoff double. The gutsy hurler then settled down, retiring three consecutive Red Devils' hitters. In Homer's half of the sixth, for the second straight frame, its leadoff hitter was hit by a pitch. This time it was Cody Collmenter, who was replaced on the bases by pinch runner Mason Novess. Winchell got a sacrifice bunt down to advance Novess to second base with one out. Sophomore Austin Rinard, Homer's eighth-place hitter, lined a deep single to center field to score Novess, giving the Trojans a 3-2 advantage. Homer Nation roared with applause in the packed stands. The baseball-savvy fans knew their boys were just three outs away from a second state championship.

Adrenaline pumping like crazy, Compton trotted out to the mound with the ultimate revenge at his fingertips. Holton's

7-8-9 hitters were due up in the top of the seventh. With Homer's fans going bananas, Finch made a spectacular diving catch in short right field for Holton's first out. Compton struck out the second batter, setting the stage for one final piece of history. Holton's Drew Giddings hit a ground ball to second, which Finch calmly fielded and tossed to Holcomb for the final out. Mitts flew into the air and Homer's players charged toward the mound to mob Compton and celebrate their feat.

Homer won 3-2 despite getting just four hits, two fewer than Holton. Compton struck out 10 batters, while improving his season record to 13-1 and career record to 42-3.

The victory was tremendous for everyone, but it had been necessary for Compton. Salow said it was his dream to have the ball back in Compton's hands after what happened the year before. "It's been topsy-turvy, emotional, and difficult," Salow said about his time with Compton. "Some days it's depressing, but in the end, it was very, very rewarding. He's a great kid."

NOTHING WAS GOING TO STOP DUSTY COMPTON FROM PITCHING IN THE FINAL GAME.
PHOTO COURTESY OF MHSAA.

And what about the line drive to the face? How did Compton shrug that off? "By the time I got to the mound, his face was already all swollen up," Salow said. "He's a gamer. I would've had to pry the ball away from him."

The emotional kid was, well, emotional after playing his last high-school baseball game. Compton lived for this stuff and he wasn't ready to give it up. He didn't want to leave the field. "My sophomore year I was almost ineligible and I thought about dropping out," Compton

SCOTT SALOW OVERCOMES WHIPPED CREAM TO TALK ABOUT ANOTHER BIG HOMER WIN.
PHOTO BY DOUG ALLEN, COURTESY OF THE BATTLE CREEK ENQUIRER

said. "[Salow] believed in me the whole time. He's a great role model for everybody and especially me. I'm really glad I had him as a coach."

Twelve seniors, including eight starters, finished their careers with a record of 143-6 and two state titles. Homer went 113-2 over the final three seasons. "What a great way to end it for these great kids," said Salow, who was 185-20 in six seasons as head coach. "They've done so many things, not only for the school but for high school baseball in Michigan. They've certainly turned Homer upside-down."

After taking four years off of coaching to spend more time with his family, Tom Salow rejoined his brother Scott as an assistant in 2005, the year Homer lost in the state final. So when the Trojans defeated Holton for the championship, it was the first one for the Salow brothers to enjoy together in the dugout. But more than personal glory, Tom Salow says, he thinks the 2006 title was important for the village at large. "I think it healed some wounds and really brought the community together," Tom said, "and we needed it because of the divisiveness from the arbitration. I saw people at games that I never thought I'd see there. It was a real 'Hoosiers' moment, with the people pouring out and talking about it. Just a real neat experience."

Mike Warner, the *Homer Index* editor who had been at so many of the games over the years, said the 2006 title is one that will always stick in his memory. "There was just so much pressure on those kids," Warner said. "It's hard to go into a season knowing that anything less than a state title would be a failure. They ran out of gas that last week, they didn't play their best ball during the last week. It was more on heart than anything else. That epitomized those kids."

C.J. Finch said: "That put an exclamation point at the end of our careers. Without that, I would've felt that all the things we did accomplish would've been lessened without another state title our senior year. It was the end of Homer baseball for me and the end of Homer baseball for all my great friends on the team. It was kind of depressing knowing I wouldn't step on the field with all of them anymore."

>>><<<

The era was over but there was one last honor for Homer baseball to enjoy. Around midnight after Homer's semifinal win over Rochester Hills Lutheran Northwest, Salow received a call that woke him up out of bed. On the other end was Bad Axe High School baseball coach Wayne Turmell, who proceeded to tell Salow that he had a dilemma. Turmell was president of the Michigan High School Baseball Coaches Association, and his group had a predicament it had never encountered before.

With the state championship game merely hours away, Turmell told Salow that both Dale Cornstubble and Dan Holcomb had been named co-Mr. Baseball in the state of Michigan. The problem was that the award was presented on Monday after the state championship games at a banquet in Detroit, where all the players from the Michigan High School All-Star Baseball Game would be present. (The game was Tuesday at Comerica Park, home of the Detroit Tigers.) Only one player per high-school team was allowed to play in the All-Star game, and Homer's representative was Cornstubble. Turmell told Salow he'd have to somehow get Holcomb to attend the banquet without telling him why.

After Homer won the state championship over Holton, Salow took Holcomb aside and said he should go to the All-Star banquet to support his best friend and teammate, Cornstubble. Ever the loyal friend, Holcomb said that would be fine. So

Salow, wife Cammy, Tom Salow, and the Holcombs drove to Detroit to watch Cornstubble get honored as a All-Star representative. Neither player knew what would come next.

Sitting among the 30 or so other All-Stars, Cornstubble was announced as the recipient of the 2006 Mr. Baseball Award. When Homer's catcher reached the podium he glanced at the award and then found Holcomb in the crowd. "I'm sitting there and Dale just smiles at me. He gives me this little cheesy smile," said Holcomb, who went 15-0 with a 0.73 ERA and 147 strikeouts in 77 innings as a senior. "Then they called me up there and showed me the award and it was just, 'Wow.' We didn't think we were going to get it, it's usually somebody from the Detroit area. But to get it with your best friend is just unreal. It was unbelievable. You couldn't ask for a better ending."

"When I saw Dan got it, that made it 10 times better," said Cornstubble, who hit .500 with 12 home runs, 50 RBI, and 12 baserunners thrown out from his catcher position. "It's awesome. I always thought about it but I didn't think I'd receive it."

It was quite a week for Salow, who was only 48 hours removed from hoisting his second state title trophy in three years. "I thought a couple of our kids might crack the top 10," Salow said. "I just didn't think they'd give it to a small school."

There it was. The last piece of hardware for Cornstubble and Holcomb. Two state championships. Seventy-five straight wins, setting a national record. Countless moments of civic pride that can't be measured by numbers. And lastly, two best friends, sharing the top award for high school baseball players in Michigan. It was the perfect ending to a glorious three-year ride that will never be forgotten.

Epilogue

After going 31-1 as a high school pitcher, Josh Collmenter didn't receive a Division 1 scholarship offer until the very end of his senior season. Whether it was his funky over-the-top throwing motion or a small-school bias, the colleges weren't all that intrigued. Central Michigan finally did offer, and it didn't take long to realize what a steal he was. The once-pudgy kid quickly grew into a man at CMU, and by the end of his freshman season he had made 10 starts, going 7-1 with a 2.70 ERA and 77 strikeouts in 90 innings. It was enough to earn Collmenter a place on the Louisville Slugger Freshman All-America team and a second-team All-Mid American Conference selection.

As a sophomore, Collmenter was a fixture in the starting rotation, and though his win-loss mark slipped to 8-5, he still struck out 94 batters in 95 innings and had a very respectable 3.41 ERA. By this point, he was becoming a known prospect. Collmenter was invited to play in the prestigious Cape Cod Summer Baseball League, where he pitched for the Hyannis (Mass.) Mets. In the Cape Cod, a veritable training ground for the minor leagues, he went 1-1 with a 2.41 ERA.

The 6-4, 235-pound Collmenter was clearly CMU's No. 1 pitcher by his junior season in 2006. Sporting a scruffy beard that befitted his easygoing personality, Collmenter dominated as a junior. He went 9-4 with a 1.93 ERA, including 8-1 with a 0.71 ERA in conference games, leading the league in nearly every pitching category. It earned him MAC Pitcher of the Year, All-Mideast Region first team and a spot on *Base-*

ball America's third-team All-America list. Rumors abounded that Collmenter could be selected as high as the fifth round of the Major League Draft, which he became eligible for after his junior season.

With a fastball that occasionally reaches 90, but is often as fast in the seventh inning as the first, and a pretty good curveball and changeup, Collmenter was viewed simply as a guy who "knows how to pitch." That trait isn't valued as high by major-league scouts as throwing gas in the upper 90s, but it was enough for the Arizona Diamondbacks to select Collmenter in the 15th round of the 2007 MLB draft. With a 3.8 GPA and nearing his marketing degree, Collmenter was eager to move on to the next challenge. He signed with the Diamondbacks for $80,000 and made his professional baseball debut on July 16, 2007, with the Yakima (Wash.) Bears of the short-season Northwest League.

Following a brief adjustment period, Collmenter did what he always has done: won games. Starting 12 games for Yakima, Collmenter tied for the team lead with six wins (he was 6-3) and had a 2.71 ERA. He also struck out 57 batters in 66 ⅓ innings. Collmenter started the 2008 season in the Low-A Midwest League, where the South Bend (Ind.) Silverhawks are the Diamondbacks' affiliate. South Bend is only about 90 minutes from Homer, meaning Collmenter will have a terrific local following.

The journey has been enjoyable for the player who started Homer baseball on the path to prominence. "Coming from a small town was definitely a disadvantage," Collmenter said. "But just to see how far I've come along, so far everything's worked out for the best. To say my job is playing baseball is great because I have so much fun going to the ballpark."

Collmenter still returns to Homer in the offseason and goes back to his old school occasionally to visit with Salow. He enjoys the fact he helped put Homer baseball on the map and opened doors for guys like Holcomb and Cornstubble to get Division 1 scholarships. He also knows what it would mean to Homer if he ever throws in a major-league game. "It would mean there probably wouldn't be anybody in Homer," he said. "It would mean a lot because we've had some good athletes come through here but no one has ever made the major leagues. Our claim to fame is an Olympic kayaker [Greg Barton] and everyone I grew up with and their parents know about him. I think they would appreciate the fact they could say they know someone pitching in the major leagues."

>>><<<

Fresh off winning Mr. Baseball, Dale Cornstubble became Central Michigan's starting catcher as a freshman where he caught most of Collmenter's games in 2007. Cornstubble excelled behind the plate as he always had, but struggled to hit college-level pitching at the beginning. His defense was enough to keep him in the lineup, though, and by the time conference play started, Cornstubble was doing more than his share of hitting in the No. 9 hole. During MAC games, Cornstubble hit

.311 with 25 RBI in 26 games, good for seventh in the league in that category.

Overall, Cornstubble hit .249 in 50 games, starting 44 of them, for the 35-21 Chippewas. CMU finished second in the MAC, incidentally falling down the stretch when the return of a once-injured veteran moved Cornstubble to the bench in favor of a better hitting lineup. Cornstubble followed his teammate Collmenter to the Hyannis Mets of the Cape Cod League after the season. He's penciled in as CMU's starting catcher for the 2008 season and by virtue of his fabulous defensive skills, is considered a candidate to be drafted in a year or two. In fact, scouts from at least a few major-league teams visited the Cornstubble home when Dale was a senior at Homer to discuss his possible draft status at the time.

>>><<<

Dan Holcomb, meanwhile, hasn't played a college game yet. In the summer after winning Mr. Baseball, Holcomb was experiencing pain in his right elbow while pitching for the Grand Rapids Diamonds. The injury required Tommy John surgery, which Holcomb had done by famed orthopedic surgeon Dr. James Andrews in Birmingham, Ala. Holcomb was awed by the framed photos and jerseys in Andrews' office (he's the Who's Who of surgeons when it comes to professional athletes) before going through the now-routine elbow surgery. Tommy John surgery, named after the former major league pitcher whom it was first performed on in 1974, is where a tendon is removed from your wrist or hamstring and grafted back into your elbow. Doctors call it a UCL, ulnar collateral ligament reconstruction, which leaves about a four-inch scar next to a patient's elbow. The procedure has been a career saver for many a pitcher, including Mariano Rivera, John Smoltz, and Erik Bedard. More than 100 major-league players have played after having the surgery, an amazing statistic considering an elbow injury often used to end pitchers' careers.

While recovering from the procedure, Holcomb sat out the 2007 season at Evansville. He got back on the mound for the first time for Evansville's fall exhibition season and said it felt okay. His velocity was not all the way back but that's typical of the timeline for Tommy John patients. Generally it takes a full year to recover and then sometimes another year after that to get back to normal. Once that occurs, it's not uncommon for pitchers to throw even harder than they originally did. A 4.0 student, Holcomb is majoring in business and he continues to be conscience about a life after baseball when his career ends. It's too early to tell if Holcomb will be a candidate to be drafted after his junior season.

Though the head coach who recruited Holcomb left for Notre Dame, the Purple Aces have high hopes for him. Evansville's coaches are hoping Holcomb will be a weekend starter (college baseball lingo for top three) in 2008 as a redshirt freshman. After that, Holcomb will come home for the summer. He has signed a contract to play for the Battle Creek Bombers of the Northwoods League in the summer of 2008, which is considered one of the top summer collegiate baseball leagues in the country. "I can't wait to get back up there," Holcomb said.

The MHSAA's pitching record book reads like a Homer baseball media guide. Holcomb finished his high school career fourth in state history in wins (45), one place behind Collmenter's 49. The state shutout record for one season is held by Josh Collmenter (13 in 2004), Dan Holcomb (9 in 2005), and Dan Holcomb (9 in 2004). Collmenter is first in career shutouts (23), Compton is third (20), and Holcomb is fourth (19). Holcomb ranks second in no-hitters in a season (5). Holcomb's eight career no-hitters are tied for first with a pitcher from the 1940s and another in the '90s. Holcomb is the only pitcher in state history with two perfect games in a single season; he and Compton are tied for first with three career perfect games. Collmenter is second in single-season strikeouts (223) in 2004. Collmenter's 546 career strikeouts are fourth in state history.

>>><<<

Unable to make the grade requirements for a Division 1 school, Dusty Compton went to Grand Rapids Community College, one of the top junior college programs in the Midwest. But as many around him feared, Compton didn't respond well to being on his own, away from friends and familiar surroundings. Depending on who you talk with, Compton was either kicked out of school or he dropped out. He never played an inning for Grand Rapids C.C. More alarmingly, high-school friends and coaches are not quite sure of Compton's whereabouts these days.

When his classmates were back for summer vacation after their freshmen years of college, there were a few Compton sightings, and he even played in a couple informal summer baseball games with the guys in a Jackson league. Somewhere along the way, his arm basically died and the former fireballer was resigned to playing the infield and hitting. Compton was supposed to transfer to Kellogg Community College in Battle Creek in 2007, but he never surfaced there either. To this day, Dusty remains the player Salow is most concerned about in the long term. Everybody hopes Dusty turns out well but his fractured family life will always have his friends worried about him.

>>><<<

Three other players got a taste of college baseball. C.J. Finch, the competitor whose name is littered all over the state record book, signed with Jackson Community College but sat out most of the year with a leg injury. Though others usually got most of the credit for Homer, Finch compiled a sensational high-school career. He finished second in state history in runs scored (243), sixth in stolen bases (140) and eighth in hits (186).

Heading into the spring of 2008, Finch was healed and looking forward to his first year of college ball at Jackson C.C. He has also signed to play at Spring Arbor in 2009, where he'll have three years of eligibility at the Salows' alma mater. Aside from being a heckuva high-school player, Finch was also one of the team's best quotes. With gems like, "Other teams knew they were playing for second place; not first," reporters couldn't resist the urge to put a microphone in front of Finch's face.

>>><<<

Ryan Thurston, the heavy-hitting shortstop, is entering his second year playing for Division 3 Albion College in Michigan. Thurston was one of the team's quietest players, a real family kid, and he too put up huge numbers that were often overlooked. Batting second in Homer's lineup, Thurston finished second in state history in grand slams (four, tied with Compton), third in career RBI (182), fifth in runs scored (197), and seventh in hits (187). (In a showing of Homer's dominance, five of the top eight career state hits leaders are Trojans: Finch, Thurston, Cornstubble, Compton, and Jeff Poe, who played from 1997-2000.)

Thurston came off the bench for Albion as a freshman, but with several players lost to graduation, he's been moved to third base and is projected to hit in the middle of the Britons' order as a sophomore.

>>><<<

Brock Winchell, the slender kid with a knack for the big postseason hit, played one year of baseball at Division 3 Adrian College in Michigan. Winchell chose to transfer after his freshman year and will likely not play college ball again.

>>><<<

After seeing the third of his three sons, Joe, graduate from Homer, superintendent Brent Holcomb decided it was time for a new challenge. Holcomb worked in Homer for 16 years, seven as middle school principal and nine as superintendent, before he took the superintendent job at Alpena High School prior to the 2007-08 school year. Alpena is in the northeast corner of Michigan's Lower Peninsula, just off of Lake Huron. Holcomb oversaw roughly 1,000 kids in K-12 at Homer; now he's in charge of looking after about 4,600 in Alpena.

Holcomb reports that Alpena is a lot like Homer in that both are blue-collar towns with friendly people. As a man squarely in the middle of the Salow-Finch controversy, Holcomb says only one thing still bothers him from that time: "The hardship that was created for Scott," Holcomb says. "He didn't deserve that. If I have any regrets, it's that I played a role in creating stress for Scott and that wasn't fair to him or his family."

"Time tends to soften your view of things," Holcomb continued. "In hindsight, all the right things happened. I always felt bad that in some ways I played a role in that whole mess. I think I shouldn't have let it happen in the first place."

>>><<<

Chuck Finch is now in his 23rd year as a teacher and coach at Homer. Since C.J. graduated, Chuck's involvement in the baseball program has dwindled. This past year, he was an assistant varsity football and eighth-grade basketball coach.

Finch's feelings about the head baseball coaching situation haven't changed. "I've pretty much moved on with the reality that the powers that be at that time manipulated the situation to get what they wanted," Finch said. "I'm still disappointed from the perspective of how that situation was handled."

Finch believes he should've been elevated to varsity assistant when the five freshmen, including C.J., were brought up to varsity. After Finch had convinced Salow to be the head coach when Tom resigned, Chuck figured it was a no-brainer to be paid back by continuing to coach the players he and Tom Sharpley had instructed since the third grade.

"After the loyalty that I had shown the baseball program all those years," Chuck said, "I won't forgive or forget the choice [Salow] made when he had a chance to reciprocate the loyalty I'd shown him."

>>><<<

As for the teachers and the union, Art Welch said some bitter feelings persist to this day. "I think there's still some scars from it," Welch said.

>>><<<

In the summer following the 2006 state championship, the team gathered one last time for a pizza party at Cascarelli's. They were all there, joking, eating and enjoying each other's company as they've done for years. Scott Salow knew this was a rare moment, as the kids would soon go their separate ways. "I challenged the kids to stay in touch with each other," Salow said. "The kids seemed to have a puzzled look on their faces when I said that. It was kind of, 'Coach, what are you saying, of course we're going to see each other.' It was extremely emotional for me. To have all these kids in the same room at the same time will be hard to do again."

Baseball carries on at Homer High School, and Salow remains in his third-base coaching box. The Trojans still run the "catcher pickoff" and still enforce the "seven-second rule." But after the special group of seniors graduated in 2006, Homer got a dose of reality the following season. They finished 20-13 and the streak of six consecutive league titles ended when Quincy took first. Homer finished third.

Thanks to the glut of attention garnered by the national win streak and state championships, Salow has benefited professionally. After he won the National Coach of the Year by the National High School Coaches Association, the Pennsylvania-based organization offered Salow a job. He's now in charge of baseball at the NHSCA, a title deemed National Baseball Executive Producer. The side job has taken him to places like San Diego and Maryland, where Salow is part of a committee that decides where national tournaments are played while helping to organize coaches' clinics. In addition, Salow is now regularly asked to speak at clinics or help at prestigious college camps, like the University of Michigan's.

Entering the 2008 season, Salow is 205-33 in seven years as Homer's coach. Thirteen of those 33 losses came in '07, the year after the greatest class in Homer history had graduated. "We weren't a very good team last year and yet we won 20 games. A lot of programs would kill for that," Salow said. "And yet I say we're 20-13 and I cringe every time I say the '13' part. It just kills me."

Austin Rinard, the sophomore right fielder on Homer's 2006 title team, will be the school's next college player. A big, strong kid, Rinard hit 10 home runs as a junior and will attend Kellogg C.C. in the fall of 2008. He hopes to play Division 1 ball after a couple years at Kellogg.

Salow says he's reminded of the great era almost every day. Whether it's people asking him on the street about a particular player or a colleague recalling a big game of yesteryear, the memory of those amazing years is always a heartbeat away. Truth be told, he doesn't want to forget.

"They gave a community, certainly our school, their parents, our coaching staff and just fans of good stories, four years of doing things the right way," Salow says with nostalgia. "They were able to provide some shining moments I don't think anyone will soon forget. Those memories you can't ever take away."

About the Author

Jeff Karzen is a sports writer at the *Battle Creek Enquirer* in Michigan. He was on the front lines of Homer's baseball run while covering the team for the *Enquirer*.

A native of Evanston, Ill., Karzen has a journalism degree from Michigan State University. His work has been featured in *Baseball America*, *Michigan History* magazine, and the Chicago Cubs' *Vine Line* magazine.

PHOTO BY DOUG ALLEN